T0157826

# Alabaster Box

## The Heart Of A Poet...

Tisha Leija

iUniverse, Inc.
Bloomington

Alabaster Box
The Heart Of A Poet ...

Copyright © 2011 Tisha Leija

iUniverse books may be ordered through booksellers or by contacting:

iUniverse
1663 Liberty Drive
Bloomington, IN 47403
www.iuniverse.com
1-800-Authors (1-800-288-4677)

ISBN: 978-1-4502-9662-5 (pbk)
ISBN: 978-1-4502-9663-2 (ebk)

Printed in the United States of America

iUniverse rev. date: 3/22/2011

# Contents

# Chapter 3: Trials

# Chapter Four: Triumphs & Inspirations

## Chapter 5: Love

*In the Bible, Mary anointed Jesus with the contents of her alabaster box. In biblical days the alabaster box held spikenard, an aromatic ointment or oil. It was a very expensive perfume, and the best that she had. Out of love, honor, respect, and complete gratitude she poured it on Jesus. Similar to Mary, I take that which is special to me, and for the same reasons...I give it to God to be used in however way He sees fit.*

*The spikenard was made with oil infused with the scents of different flowers, plants and herbs. Some of which came from far lands, the ingredients were not easy to come by. Because of this, the ointment was of great worth. Each chapter of this book represents a different ingredient in my alabaster box. I hope it blesses you, as it has blessed me.*

*Luke 7:44-50*
*44And He turned to the woman, and said unto Simon, Seest thou this woman? I entered into thine house, thou gavest Me no water for my feet: but she hath washed My feet with tears, and wiped them with the hairs of her head.45Thou gavest Me no kiss: but this woman since the time I came in hath not ceased to kiss My feet. 46 My head with oil thou didst not anoint: but this woman hath anointed My feet with ointment.47 Wherefore I say unto thee, her sins, which are many, are forgiven; for she loved much: but to whom little is forgiven, the same loveth little. 48 And he said unto her, Thy sins are forgiven.49 And they that sat at meat with him began to say within themselves, Who is this that forgiveth sins also? 50 And He said to the woman, Thy faith hath saved thee; go in peace.*

*Within Mary's alabaster box there was precious, expensive oil, called spikenard that she anointed Jesus with before He went to the cross. She expressed her love and complete willingness to submit to Him the best way she could. She gave the costliest thing she had, signifying the appreciation for the cost that He was about to pay to redeem us from death and hell. It was appropriate for Jesus to have His feet washed upon entering the house, but no one washed His feet. Mary washed them with her tears and dried them with her hair. I don't know if that was her intention. I believe as she worshipped at the Master's feet she wept, and held on to Him. As she bowed, and cried, and kissed His feet, she clung to Him all the more...*

*through the motion of her love, she did in fact wash His feet with her tears and dry them with her hair.*

*Father, I come to you unworthy by anything that I have done. Deserving death, but justified by the blood that You shed for me. Thank You for speaking to me. Thank You for speaking through me. Thank You for never leaving me & most of all… thank You for saving my soul. I know that You have already gone to Calvary, and the work was finished long ago. Still, I offer the contents of my alabaster box. I pray that the oil, the tears, and the fragrance of trials, triumphs, & love within the pages of this book will be a sweet smelling savor to You. You are Wonderful, You are everything that I'll ever need, exactly when I need it, and I am grateful.*

*I pray this book blesses every eye that reads it, and every ear that hears it… most of all, that You be glorified!!!*

*Dear Readers,*
*I sincerely thank you for taking time to read my work. I am very appreciative for all the encouragement that I have received along the way. I am truly honored to have been able to write for some of you personally. It means so much that you allowed me to write for some of the most important times of your lives. Within these pages you'll read about some of the most important times of mine. This is my journal, these are my prayers, these are thoughts, emotions, and issues that are a part of who I am…this is me. I pray that you like it, I pray that it illuminates your life in some way…and I pray that it inspires you to pick up a pen, and write! No one is a writer before they write…you have to "do" the thing in order the "be" the thing.*

*Peace and Blessings To All*
*~T. Leija*

# Chapter 1:
# Oil

*This emollient captured the aromas of the different botanicals and spices that were added to it. It was the base of every ointment, or fragrance. The perfume could not be made without oil.*

*Oil for the light, spices for anointing oil, and for sweet incense. (Exodus 25:6)*

# IN THE PALM OF YOUR HAND

*The pride of man*
*Is the prelude to his fall*
*In humility to my knees*
*I fall*
*Asking, pleading, seeking, needing...*
*Your Anointing...*
*To fall*
*Fall fresh like rain*
*I need the oil of Your Glory*
*To rush in and fill*
*Every empty place within my soul*
*Cover me in the All of You*
*I am ever amazed*
*Always in awe of You*
*Wonderful Counselor*
*The Great I AM*
*Bruised, yet Unblemished*
*Perfect in every way*
*Erase mine own iniquities*
*That I may pray*
*From a heart that's pure*
*As it beats in me...*
*Can anything pure even be in me*
*It can, if you command it to...*
*Even the wickedest of hearts*
*Will obey Your truth*
*I break free*
*From the flesh that I despise*
*Looking in my eyes*
*You'll hear my soul cry*
*Oh God...*
*Who am I*
*That You should take thought of me*
*What is man that you are mindful of him*
*I have no concern of what I should eat or drink*

*What I'll wear*
*Or where I'll sleep*
*For You have already arranged it all for me*
*I know myself to be invisible, insignificant*
*In comparison to You*
*Knowing me better than I know myself*
*You made me joint heirs with You*
*Finding me to be terrific*
*An honored vessel for Your use*
*Able to do…*
*Anything*
*For it is You, who strengthens me*
*There is no failure in You*
*And You are in me…*
*And everything is possible*
*Nothing is out of my reach*
*Suspended in mid-air*
*I stand*
*No strings attached*
*Easy I rest*
*Completely*
*In the palm of Your hand*

# THE TRUTH

*In the Beauty of who You are...*
*I worship You*
*For Your loving kindness is better than life*
*Your Love is like*
*Nothing else that exists*
*Through pure lips that speak only the truth*
*You...*
*Kissed the sky*
*Painting a portrait*
*All so my eyes*
*Could somehow gaze upon Your Glory*
*How beautiful Thou art*
*Father in the most secret place of my heart*
*Is where I find you*
*Waiting...patiently*
*Gently yielding*
*Yourself to me*
*Reaching for my lowly soul*
*Through the piercings in Your palms I am made whole*
*Lord I worship You*
*With my spirit I cry*
*Hallelujah*
*Glory to the Precious Lamb of God*
*My soul's salvation*
*My Savior*
*My Redeemer*
*The Lifter of my head*
*My Keeper*
*My reason for being*
*Even the air that I'm breathing belongs*
*To You*
*The birds sing songs for You*
*The leaves on trees blown by the breeze*
*Wave like flags of surrender*
*Rendering praise to Your Holy Name*
*You are Alpha and Omega*

*The Sacrificial Lamb*
*The Risen Savior*
*And my soul cries*
*Hallelujah*
*Glory to the KING*
*KING of Kings, LORD of Lords*
*Who could ever ask for more…*
*Lord, I need you now*
*I press pass distractions*
*I push thru despair*
*I bind the confusion that lingers in the air*
*And I reach for You*
*That I may hold on to*
*The only Source*
*The One Force that has held me*
*Before the beginning*
*Previous to the introduction of time*
*You knew me before I was*
*You made me Yours…*
*All so You could be mine*
*And I'm grateful*
*Without You*
*There is no place that I can go*
*You are my Melody*
*I can't sing without You*
*You are in my every thought…I can't help but think about you*
*You're every Word to every poem*
*That I'll ever write*
*Without You*
*Nothing is right*
*Without You, the sun won't shine*
*The wind won't blow*
*Rain won't fall*
*Flowers won't grow*
*You are in everything*
*All of it is You*
*You are the Purest, Loveliest, most Wonderful*
*Holiest*
*You, Dear God are the Truth*

## MY FATHER

*My Father woke me this morning…so gentle and sweet*
*He tossed the petals of roses at my feet*
*He blew kisses to me… that felt like wind*
*Not only is He my Father…*
*He's my very best friend*
*His smile is my sunshine…*
*And when He winks His eye*
*It's like the twinkle of the stars*
*In the midnight sky*
*So that I could bathe…*
*For me, He made seas*
*He went to the depths of hell*
*And took back the keys…*
*Now, I will never be locked out of my dreams*
*Because I am in Him, and He is in me*
*I can speak words that will shape, carve, and create my destiny*
*My Father is wonderful…He's perfect no doubt*
*When I fall into trouble…He pulls me right out*
*Never do I have to worry, fret, or fear…*
*Never am I lonely…He is ever near*
*He cries with me…through joy and pain*
*His tears fall down in the form of rain*
*They water my spirit, my heart and soul*
*Without Him I'm incomplete…*
*With Him I'm whole*
*He is the GREAT I AM…& I realize this means…*
*I am a child of the KING of Kings*
*This is no story, fairytale, or cliché…*
*I am joint heirs with Christ every single day*
*Now what exactly does that mean…*
*Through Him, I can simply do ALL things!*

## SHAKE THE GATES

*I want to shake the gates of hell*
*Stand on Lucifer's doorstep ringing his bell*
*And have him too scared to answer*
*I wanna write poetry so powerful, when read, spoken, heard, or held*
*It'll cure cancer, wipe away AIDS, illness, and disease*
*I wanna write to ease the discomfort and miseries*
*I wanna be the missing piece, to solve every un-solved mystery*
*I won't repeat history, when there's a promising future ahead of me*
*I wanna bind defeat, and set liberty free*
*I wanna take the freedom of speech*
*And freely speak…I wanna declare war on the enemy*
*I de-clare-war…I wanna put on the whole armor of God*
*Prepared to fight*
*I don't want you to hear my poem…*
*I want you to see His light, and how bright*
*It shines…to remind us that perfect love casts out fear*
*As a glimmer of light destroys darkness, a gentle answer*
*Will soften the heart's hardness…making it easier to hear…Jesus*
*I hear Jesus sayin', "I'm on My way and, no man knows the hour or day*
*Just be ready…quick-get-ready*
*Let the pen be your sword, the paper your shield*
*Through rhythmic words and lyrical lines speak forth My perfect will*
*For you are sent as a warning, a storm is coming*
*Some will mock, some will scorn, none will say they weren't forewarned*
*The deaf hear Me, the blind see Me…*
*The dead breathe, and cry tears for they believe Me*
*The mute speak, and praise My Name, the lame leap, and do the same*
*The simple hear and understand, the paralyzed stand, and lift their hands*
*Those who were suicidal, live*
*…and preach life*
*The atheist, lifts his eyes to Christ*
*He'll fall on his knees as he hears Me speak*
*"…I've been here the whole time.*
*I have been here the whole time"*

*And that's why you write…*
*Not for fortune, nor for fame, but to magnify and bring glory to My Name*
*You'll write poems that turn murdering spirits into repentant souls*
*You'll speak forth, and tell truths untold*
*You'll uncover the hidden things that no one knows*
*It'll baffle their minds, they'll wonder…how did she know*
*Only the blessed will see*
*These words are not you, but an extension of Me*
*Through parables I speak, through poetry I reach*
*For every ear that hears…*
*Which really listens to Me*

# REPENTANCE

*Father, again I come to you*
*Stumbling and feeling my way*
*Like a child in the dark*
*The enemy is throwing darts*
*And, they are penetrating my heart*
*I'm so tired of traveling the same road*
*And winding up in the same mess*
*God forgive me, and equip me*
*To pass this test*
*Trials on every side*
*I'm whipped by the winds of a storm so strong*
*I fall to my knees sobbing for I have nothing...*
*At least nothing but Your Word to stand on*
*And in the middle of my tears I begin to think of Your every promise*
*And how You haven't failed me yet*
*The more I remember the awe of You*
*The more my problems I forget*
*Jesus, if I don't have anyone in this world*
*That's alright*
*Cuz all I'll ever need, I have in You*
*Father perfect my walk, and edify my talk*
*Daily transform me*
*That what You have done*
*I may also do*

# DENIAL

*I am her*
*You are me*
*She is you*
*They are us*
*We are them*
*Who among men*
*Are perfect*
*Which of us are better than the other*
*Who can look deeper than color*
*Who can see past gender and remember*
*Just as we all were born*
*We all must die*
*Who can feel love and pain*
*And not cry*
*Who would rather*
*Bypass the truth*
*To succumb to a lie*
*In denial*
*Denying the fact*
*That issues ain't white or black*
*Truthfully, there is a lack*
*Of self esteem*
*Meaning…*
*We'd rather point out everybody else's wrongs*
*As an excuse to make our sins*
*Appear right*
*We're denying the fact that we ain't right*
*There is no time*
*We're out of time*
*Yet we search for more*
*Of that which we have not*
*We're half cold and half hot*
*Positioned in the perfect spot*
*To get spewed out the mouth*
*Of God…*

*And that ain't what we want*
*Most of us know what to do…*
*But we don't*
*Cuz neighbor lovin'*
*And brother keepin'*
*Is more of an inconvenience*
*Then a blessin'*
*Hell is where we headed*
*With our church clothes on*
*We always talkin' about what ain't right in the world*
*Never mentioning the fact that we are what's wrong*
*I mean God said that life and death is in the power of the tongue*
*I refuse to be guilty of murdering verbally*
*Or any way otherwise*
*If we could see ourselves through God's eyes*
*What would the vision be*
*I mean can you imagine the moment His foot hits the earth*
*And you must give an account for all of your work*
*Or lack of, in some cases*
*What the saints gone say when*
*He wanna know how come more folk ain't saved*
*"No God, we didn't witness to them*
*But when we passed them in sin*
*We prayed*
*We bowed our heads and said*
*Have Your way"*
*Not knowing we didn't have another day*
*Before we would be face to face with Thee*
*The KING of Kings*
*Oh God forgive us all*
*For we did fall*
*Short of Your glory*
*We heard about the story…*
*But never really read it*
*I know it was something about*
*Oil in lamps*
*And being a light*
*I heard about a housetop*

*And a thief in the night*
*I might not have it all right…*
*I didn't read the book*
*But I did see The Passion of Christ*
*So I know that gotta count for somethin'*
*Don't it*
*I mean I was gonna do Your will*
*And keep all Your commandments*
*You gotta understand it's*
*Not easy*
*Dealin' with this flesh*
*I can't be held accountable for all my actions…*
*That devil is a mess…*
*Ain't he, Jesus*
*You must agree*
*Didn't You tell us that the flesh is weak*
*And we, parish for lack of knowledge*
*Or is our failure unbelief*
*I believe I'm guilty until pardoned innocent*
*No way to escape judgment's trial*
*Nobody knows when the clock stops*
*But when the last tics toc*
*Don't get caught…*
*In denial*

# BEING HONEST WITH GOD

*I wonder what would happen if we told God the truth*
*Instead of always lyin'*
*What would happen if we went to Him sayin'*
*Father, I really ain't tryin'*
*I have no desire to get along with my brothers*
*And I don't even like my neighbors*
*I had spare change*
*But I didn't give it to the man who asked cuz*
*I need somebody to do me a favor*
*God I do want to get married and settle down*
*I just haven't found the time to stop sleepin' around*
*I do want a husband*
*But there's lust in*
*My heart*
*And I don't mean for it to be*
*But nobody ever dealt with the seeds*
*Of insecurity*
*That blossomed promiscuity in my youth*
*I just want to lay it all out before You*
*I need to expose myself*
*I'm desperate for help*
*I'm tired of hiding behind the fact that I'm saved*
*I sing, shout, talk in tongues and I pray out loud*
*And I ain't free*
*Cuz part of me don't want to confess all my sin*
*Cuz then I'm accountable*
*For actions worthy of death*
*Insurmountable*
*Places, times and various events*
*I could have repented*
*But I didn't*
*Cuz I'm not finished*
*Gettin' high*
*I'm not perfect*
*And I don't want to pretend to be*

Lord, I have some same gender tendencies
Not to mention
I'm prideful about my appearance and my accomplishments
As if I had anything to do with it
I've lied, cheated, been sneaky, and under handed
I've demanded things that I wasn't even entitled to
I'm trying to
Rid myself of filth through truth
God, I'm sorry
I can't hardly lift my hands
Without conviction...
I'm just tired of pretendin'
To be doin' my best
When the truth is, I'm a lazy mess
Life and death is in the power of the tongue
I've never touched a gun
Still I'm a murderer
Cuz instead of uplifting
I've used my words for killing
Back stabbing, fault finding, finger pointing
No anointing...Cuz I ain't meditated on no type of word
I'm still livin' off the sermon I heard - last week
I know I should be humble and meek
But I'm arrogant and boastful
Not hopeful...more doubting than Thomas ever was
Cussin' folks out just because
They pushed all my buttons, and flipped all my switches
I want a relationship, I'm tired of being religious
God I want to know You
So I gotta willingly show You
Everything You already see
I'm not deserving, I know I'm unworthy
I'm just askin'
Have mercy on me
I say that I trust You...
But I don't
I said I'll live for You
But I won't...

*At least not until I tell You the truth*
*There are some shameful things from my youth*
*That I'm still holdin' on to*
*I haven't forgiven people who hurt me*
*I'm still hurting...*
*Still placing blame, still calling names*
*Still ashamed of so many things that I've done*
*I wish I could run, but where can I go*
*I've done things that I don't want to admit*
*But You already know*
*I'll never know... why you kept me*
*If I were You I would of let me*
*Go...when I tried to*
*Suicidal...and You held me*
*Filthy, and You hugged me*
*Guilty and You loved me*
*Never have You judged me...*
*But You called me friend*
*Adopted me, took me in*
*You shed blood pure and innocent*
*For the remission of my sins*
*Still, I stepped out of Your will*
*Trifflin' livin'*
*God speak to me, say anything...*
*He whispered...*
*ALL- IS- FORGIVEN*

# TEACH ME TO DANCE

*Father, teach me to dance*
*Let me stand on Your feet*
*While You hold my hands*
*You are my Father*
*And I am Your child*
*I'll worship and praise You all the while*
*For there is none like You*
*You're Awesome indeed*
*Just hold my hands*
*While I stand on Your feet*
*Twirl me like a leaf in the wind*
*Like the earth on it's axis…*
*Cause me to spin*
*Toss me, tumble me, turn me around*
*Lift me high in the air*
*And gently put me down*
*Show me how I should move my arms*
*What ever way pleases You most*
*Dance with me always, be my partner for life*
*Forever hold me close*
*Teach me how to glide with grace*
*Choreograph every step*
*It's through my dance*
*That I worship Thee*
*I dance for You*
*And no one else*

## MY GIFT

God gave to me an awesome Gift, the most wonderful Gift of all
He said that it would ease my pain, and cushion my every fall
It didn't come in fancy wrap, there were no buttons or bows
Though ordinary in appearance, this Gift everyone knows
It's Gentle, Wise, with Strength unmatched
Meek and, oh so Mild
The only way to receive this Gift
Is to come just as a child
This Gift is small enough to fit in the world
While holding the world in His hand
This awesome Gift of which I speak…
Is none other than the Son of man
You see, there were no satin ribbons
A robe and sandals at best
Peek just beyond the outer appearance…
You'll see God Himself
Wrapped in flesh
I treasure this gift above any other
For there is nothing else like Christ
They ripped and tore His fleshly covering
Exposing eternal life
This Gift was hung upon a tree
Holding all the world's sin
Precious blood to cleanse my filth
Poured through perfect pierced skin
What can I give in return for this Gift, It's price I could never afford
He held my face in nail print palms…
"This is so I can have you forevermore
You see My child, there is none like you
For you were formed in the image of Me
Your soul was stolen, and up for grabs…
I bought you back on Calvary
For there is no pain worse than that
When you were snatched from Me
What better gift could I ever ask…
For I have you eternally."

# BELIEVE

*Who drives the wind*
*What force unseen*
*Who put waves in water*
*And leaves on trees*
*The answer will come*
*If you only believe*
*Who hung the stars in midnight's sky*
*Who saw the secret tears you cried*
*To every locked door...Who is the Master Key*
*I tell you, it is I*
*If you only believe*
*I am rarely understood, not easily explained*
*For only I can bring joy in the midst of pain*
*I am oceans of peace in drops of rain*
*When the way is dim*
*And you can hardly see*
*I'll be your eyes*
*If you only believe*
*It takes a little faith...the size of a mustard seed*
*I can change any situation*
*If you only believe*
*I've healed the sick, I've raised the dead*
*A crown of thorns rested upon My head*
*By My stripes, you have the victory*
*It is yours for the taking*
*If you only believe*
*If you ever want to know what a miracle is...*
*Look not with your eyes, but your heart to see*
*What is impossible for man...is easy for Me*
*I will never leave nor forsake you*
*I am every thing that you need*
*Try My favor, & test My goodness*
*If only you believe.*

## HEALING PRAYER

*I said a prayer this morning*
*I knelt quietly and still…*
*I didn't say a lot of words*
*I just asked God to heal*
*I asked that He remove your hurt*
*And every bit of pain, I asked Him to restore your health*
*And all your strength maintain*
*I didn't know all the words to say*
*I couldn't tell Him how you feel*
*But I know that God is faithful and good…*
*So I asked Him to touch and heal*
*I know there's nothing too hard*
*He is Almighty, and All Knowing*
*And that's what makes Him God*
*He made the lame walk…the deaf hear…*
*And the blind see*
*He healed the sick, raised the dead, He helped the mute to speak*
*I thanked Him for all these wonderful things*
*For you, I asked He do the same*
*On bended knee I prayed this prayer…*
*"God, heal in Jesus' Name"*

# END TIMES

*When wisdom speaks*
*It's best you listen*
*As it invites*
*You to insights*
*Of a sinful souls remission*
*Clarifying visions*
*That were too blurred to view*
*Political images misconstrued*
*No way to un-do*
*The biblical truth*
*Yet we try to out smart*
*He who was before the creation of the stars*
*Wars I ain't tryin' to start...*
*But it really ain't about republican or democrat*
*It ain't about Hussein or Arafat*
*It's not even about Bush*
*Pushin' to make legal*
*Everything that's evil*
*Hiddin' behind the American flag*
*As he brags on "We the people"*
*How are we the United States*
*When our land lacks unity*
*It's us against them*
*And you against me*
*Grown men playin' like kids*
*And I'm watchin' wondering what part of the game is this*
*They changed all the rules*
*The good guys aren't suppose to be crooks too*
*It use to*
*Be cops and robbers*
*Now the cops are the robbers*
*The cowboys and the Indians*
*Share one chief*
*They've become brethren*
*Among men whom*

*There are no rivals*
*What's scariest is that*
*We're supplying the terrorist*
*With the rifles*
*That are coincidentally*
*Aimed at us*
*As the price of petroleum*
*Inconspicuously creeps up*
*It ain't no mystery*
*You would foreknow*
*The unknown*
*If you would of checked*
*Your history*
*I'm speaking biblically*
*We have romanticized the idea of*
*A complete euphoria*
*A universal utopia*
*But our twisted whorish ways*
*Dug our own graves*
*As we paid…*
*To sleep with the enemy*
*We think it's*
*Lovely to live in the lavish land of the free*
*But freedom is a technicality*
*When economically and politically*
*You and me…*
*Gettin' screwed*
*We've been played like video games*
*And the true crime is the fact that we are victims…*
*Of generational rape*
*Babies conceived in love of hate*
*Looking through the window of rhymes*
*I stand speechless staring at…*
*The end times*

## JESUS

*In a world of millions*
*For moments...*
*It is You and I alone*
*Everything stops when I kneel at Your throne*
*You are the Alpha, the Omega*
*The Beginning and the End is You*
*You are the Creator of everything*
*Your Word is the World's only truth*
*You are too great for me to understand*
*Too powerful for me to ignore*
*A love such as Yours*
*None has known before*
*The King's court, I can't enter*
*Without permission*
*Yet the KING of kings*
*Shed His blood for me...*
*My sinful soul's remission*
*All so I could be close*
*To You*
*Before I reach for you...*
*You reach for me*
*You hold me close when I let you go*
*I don't even know the things I think I have knowledge of*
*I know not the expansion of Your love*
*Yet You grant wisdom to me*
*Freely You give*
*The costliest gift*
*The price, paid with Your blood*
*You didn't have to do it...*
*Nothing about me was right, or pure*
*Nothing in me was true*
*Yet, You looked beyond the ugliness of who I am*
*And saw the beauty of You*
*You saw Yourself in me*
*Inside of a beggar there stood a King*

*Inside of a shell so battered and bruised*
*You saw something that You could use*
*You wrapped me in mercy*
*Clothed me in grace*
*Picked me up from the muck and the mire*
*Sat me in a holy place*
*You sent rain to wash the dirt from my face*
*A mighty wind rushed me*
*Violent, fierce, and fast*
*You blew away the remnants*
*The debris from my past*
*In an instant You freed me*
*From bondage, from chains, from curses carried*
*Through generations*
*You opened Revelations*
*And revealed to me*
*Secrets that not even dreamers have seen*
*It was You who*
*Created the sun*
*And the moon*
*The mountains and stars are reflections of You*
*You are all together lovely*
*Too beautiful for my eyes*
*Your majesty and power*
*Too great for my mind*
*I don't know the words*
*I can't say anything that You*
*Haven't already heard…*
*All I know is that You are*
*God*
*And God is Love*
*All I know is I never wanna be who I once was*
*I don't even know You the way I think I do*
*Forgive me for times I've offended You*
*Who am I but flesh, and bone*
*Made from dirt and mud*
*What am I, Oh God…without Your blood*
*The blood that stains me*

It sustains me, it keeps me from being guilty
And I am grateful
Thankful
Beyond expression
Let the tears in my eyes
Be my heart's reflection
For no one knows
The thoughts that I think
The dreams that I dream
The things that I say and do
People can think what they want of me
But nothing is hidden from You
Yet not one time
Have You given up on me
Never have You thrown me away
You have every right to banish me from Your sight...
But You give me new mercy everyday
So I stand in Your presence
Unworthy by my own actions
By my own deeds...
Deserving death
You allow me to speak
Rhythmic words
Praising You with all my breath
My speech, I can speak
I can touch, taste, hear and see
I have the activity of my limbs
My hands and my feet
I have a heart in my chest that
Doesn't miss a beat
I am worth so much more than what I'll ever really know
I am greater than what I see...
You looked past my flesh and saw Yourself
Royalty uninhibited by the filth of me
And I wish my testimony could be...
I'm saved, sanctified and filled with the Holy Ghost
But mine is knowing that between You and I...
It was You who loved me most

*Sometimes I chose…*
*Not to obey*
*I made a conscious decision*
*To go my own way*
*To seek and search*
*Set my sight on all that I could see*
*When I wandered too far*
*And night got too dark*
*You left the light on, and the door unlocked for me*
*Beyond unimaginable height is Your greatness*
*Beneath the lowest part of depth is Your love*
*Surpassing the borders of eternity's width*
*Your forgiveness spans*
*More than enough for every woman, child and man*
*You are the Sovereign God, Creator, Lord and King*
*At the end of the day*
*After all my mistakes…*
*In the simplest form of who You are…*
*I find that You're Father to me…*

# A CHILD OF THE KING

*I am a God seek-er, a peace keep-er*
*A seed sow-er, A good fruit grow-er*
*A consecrated pray-er, A giant slay-er*
*A mountain move-er, a commandment do-er*
*A bible read-er, a Christ believe-er*
*A milk and honey eat-er, a devil defeat-er*
*An anointing carry-er, a cross bear-er*
*A water walk-er, a tongue talk-er*
*A dancing praise-er, a demon chase-er*
*A worship sing-er*
*A good news bring-er*
*An earth salt-er, a fire walk-er*
*A lion den sleep-er, a joy keep-er*
*A light shine-er, a victory find-er*
*A promise land posses-er, a sin confess-er*
*A brother forgive-er, an eternal live-er*
*I am a child of the KING*

# I AM

*To the hopeless, I AM Hope*
*To the helpless, I AM Help*
*To the deaf, I AM Sound*
*For the lost, I AM Found*
*For the blind, I AM Sight*
*For those in darkness, I AM Light*
*I AM Freedom, For the captive*
*I AM in everything that happens*
*For the tired, I AM Rest*
*I AM Joy for the depressed*
*Peace for the stressed, I liberate the oppressed*
*I AM GOD*
*I AM Healing, for those who hurt*
*I AM Comfort, for the grieving*
*All you have to do to receive Me*
*Is believe ME*
*I AM the Truth in a world of lies*
*I AM your only chance to fix all your failed tries*
*To the friendless, I AM a Friend*
*I will be with you 'til the end*
*I AM not a man that I should lie*
*I AM GOD*
*I AM Shelter in the midst of a storm*
*I speak peace to the wind*
*And make the seas calm*
*I AM GOD*
*I AM Bread for the hungry*
*I AM Water for all who thirst*
*I AM the Last, I AM the First…*
*I AM GOD*

## IN YOUR PRESENCE

*God, I just want to get lost in You*
*Where there is no fear*
*Frustration and doubt don't exist*
*Every arrow that's shot*
*Is sure to miss*
*God I want to dwell in the very presence of where You are*
*I need to feel the warmth of Your Love*
*It's my soul's motivation*
*I just want to be tangled up in the All of You*
*I am simply in awe of You*
*My soul is tender*
*At the mention*
*Of your name*
*I cry tears that I can't fully comprehend*
*I just know that You are nothing*
*Like men*
*You are not able to lie*
*Never will You leave me disappointed*
*Not only have you set me free*
*But You've given me an anointing*
*Appointing me to speak forth the same things that*
*You've said*
*I am humbly unworthy*
*Yet honored beyond*
*Imagination*
*With no hesitation*
*Father, I worship You*
*Wishing I could give You something*
*Anything*
*All I have is me*
*And I'm already Yours*
*What can I do*
*To show You how much*
*I adore*
*You*

*I love You*
*Still that's not enough*
*For compared to the*
*Depth, and width and height of Yours…*
*Whatsoever is my love*
*Father, my desire is to be lost in You*
*Where sin and sickness*
*Can't find me*
*I want to be in a place*
*Where I can feel Your smile, like the warmest sunshine*
*Resting upon my face*
*Lord, in Your presence is where I have to be found*
*Where darkness can not abound*
*Only in Your presence is the fullness of joy*
*I need Your peace…*
*All understanding it passes*
*Father, I come*
*Only one thing asking*
*That I may forever be in Your presence*
*Holy God it's You that I reverence*
*Truly I believe*
*That You are a rewarder to those who*
*Diligently seek*
*Daily, I'll search for You more*
*Asking that my prize be…*
*To spend every day that I breathe…*
*And all of eternity…*
*In the beauty of*
*Your presence*

# WHAT IF

*What if we live life relentless…*
*Operate without conscious*
*Never repenting*
*Not representing*
*Christ…*
*Cuz, we gotta live our life…*
*Right?*
*After all, this is our life…*
*It's the gift that God gave*
*For us the world He made…*
*Right?*
*But… what if…*
*What if the sky cracks*
*And daylight turns black*
*What if blood covers the moon*
*And the only Son is He who "was" coming soon…*
*But instantly He has appeared*
*What if it's trumpets that you hear*
*Unable to ignore the inevitable*
*Spirit intangible*
*Has manifested itself in…flesh*
*He who gave His last breath…took it back*
*And now He's back…*
*Just like He said*
*What if it happens like this and we get*
*No more time*
*He said He was coming like a thief in the night*
*No man will know the hour*
*What if we live life vicariously*
*Never respecting His power*
*Never stepping over into His truth*
*Trying to preserve our youth*
*We become aged by the years of sin*
*The residue of what we've done has deeply stained our skin*
*What if we make plans for a future that we'll never see*

*What if the last breath we breathe*
*Will be the next one we take*
*What if this world's last tomorrow*
*Happens to be today*
*What would you say*
*What could you say*
*If Jesus should ask*
*"What was more important that Me, why did you put Me last?"*
*What if He just wanted to know*
*"Why wouldn't you go...*
*Where I instructed you*
*Why did you think you were indestructible*
*Invincible*
*Pretending to...*
*Be Me"*
*What if God told you the things He showed you*
*In dreams...*
*Were actually reality*
*What if you realize all this time...You've always heard His voice*
*And the way you lived was all your choice*
*Nothing by fate or circumstance*
*Nothing at all happens by chance*
*But in the middle of the song*
*You traded partners and danced...*
*With the enemy*
*What if you realize everyday you choose your own eternity*
*What if the hell you doubted even existed*
*Is the same one in which you've eternally enlisted*
*What happens then*
*Who rescues you when*
*Flames sear your soul and*
*Destroy your flesh*
*And you realize you'll forever live in your death*
*What if you decide tomorrow you'll make a fresh*
*Start...*
*But just before the break of day*
*Cease to beat...your heart*
*For we always think we have more time*

*How can we have that which isn't ours*
*Us possessing time...Is like us catching stars*
*What is it that we fear we're giving up*
*What are we afraid to lose*
*If the next 10 seconds are not in your existence...*
*Then right now you need to choose*
*Life with Christ...you win*
*Life without Him...you lose*
*What if knowing the truth changed the choices you made*
*Romans 10:9 says if you confess Jesus with your mouth*
*And believe God raised Him from the dead*
*Then you too will be saved*
*What if you hear that and still not turn from your wicked ways...*
*The choice is yours, your decision to make*
*What if death we never have a chance to face...*
*Instead instantly we're staring into His*
*And we must face... Him*
*Can't calculate the time wasted*
*On debates of Him*
*Belief or Unbelief*
*Jew or Greek*
*Slave or free...*
*Gentile...This is the Man-Child*
*Of God*
*The One we read about, or heard about, or talked about*
*How He walked about...*
*The earth*
*How He equated our worth by His love for us*
*The same One who shed His blood for us*
*Who gave us All, yet we thought it wasn't enough...*
*What if we stop being deceived long enough to open our eyes*
*And see...*
*The only division should be saints and sinners*
*Why the gap between all God's children*
*Baptist, GOGIC, Protestant, Methodist*
*Practice this...*
*"Love one another as I have loved you."*
*Catholics, Non- Denomination*

*If you would agree to be one body…*
*You would dominate the nation*
*A family feud is the enemy's tool*
*Using ignorance as a spark…and discord as fuel*
*The air panics as the roar of terror rips through*
*Unable to decipher who it belongs to…*
*We know the devil is wicked*
*But the Word also tells us*
*God is Holy, full of compassion, slow to anger…*
*In the same breath…*
*Terrible and Jealous*
*The bible says it*
*I didn't understand it the first time I read it*
*Sounds kind of scary…don't it?*
*The devil is an angel that has fallen from grace*
*He's our enemy…*
*Who can be God's opponent*
*Satan flaunts the world like he owns it*
*The only power he has is that which God gave*
*What if today the right decision you make*
*What if you realize your purpose in life*
*Is to know that everything in existence is inferior to Christ*
*What if you feel the need to tell somebody*
*Knowing you were created just to help somebody*
*What if*
*He decided on a white horse, to come ridin'*
*And before we realized the beginning of the end*
*It was all over before it had a chance to begin*

## GOD I WANT YOU TO CHANGE ME

God I want You to change me
Dismantle my heart, take me apart…
Completely rearrange me
Refresh my spirit and soul
I need you to water every place that's dry
My cry
Is that you break me
In order to make me whole
Cuz I'm tired of being filled
With emptiness
No room for the All of You to dwell
God it's me again reaching toward Heaven
Daily running from hell
Tossing my cares where ever they may
Restless in the wind
Repenting for iniquities
Relentless to men…
Asking You wash me from all this sin
Everything that so easily besets…
Bind the faults and fears, the doubt and regrets
Just let me breathe
Let me inhale
It was in hell that You took the keys
Eternally freeing me from
Damnation of which I was deserving
God sanctify me, set me apart
No longer unrighteous and unworthy
Before I asked, I know that You heard me
For it was my soul that You redeemed
God free me from the filth of self
Only You can make me clean
So here I stand in the need of prayer…
Naked before Thine eyes
See every part, and show all to me
That I too, might be wise

*Teach me Father, all Thy ways*
*Help me run this race*
*Coach me God in such a way*
*That when it's over We're Face to face*
*A tear from Your eye will hit the sweat from my brow*
*After I've run my longest mile*
*I wanna hear You say "I'm proud of you…*
*And I'm glad that you're My child."*

# WALKING WITH GOD

*I walked and talked with God today*
*All the way to work*
*I thanked Him for being my protection*
*And healing all my hurt*
*I thanked the Father for being faithful*
*And never letting me fall*
*I told Him, out of everything…*
*I loved Him most of all*
*I told God when I woke this morning*
*There were concerns upon my heart*
*We're facing a strike in bad economy…*
*Lord, fix all that's falling apart*
*My head hung low, for I was deep in thought*
*My words were those of a child*
*"Jesus", I said…"I need a favor…*
*I haven't asked for anything big in a while"*
*When I said it, instantly I realized…*
*Nothing He does is small*
*Everything that exists…only does because HE IS*
*The Master, and Creator of it all*
*I thought of the tiniest thing He's ever done…in my prayer to mention*
*The air that I breathe, that I feel but don't see…*
*Even that is beyond my comprehension*
*He told me worry won't change a thing*
*That's something only prayer and faith can do*
*He said, "Cast your cares upon Me child, for truly…*
*I care for you*
*Be not worried or dismayed*
*Because of what tomorrow may hold*
*But trust in The One who holds tomorrow*
*There is nothing beyond My control*
*I AM not slack concerning My promises*
*Through the ages I AM Tried and True…*
*I've heard your prayers…and caught your tears…*
*There's nothing too hard for Me to do*

*I told you that joy comes in the morning*
*I wrote it upon your heart*
*If dreary is the day...and there's a forecast of rain*
*I AM still the Bright and Morning Star"*
*"God", I said..."You can do all things...*
*At once, You can work it all out."*
*"Of course I can...but as We walk in the morning...*
*What would we talk about?"*

## WEARY

*God I really need You*
*I can't just play church*
*I got a real enemy out to get me*
*And I'm dealing with some real hurt*
*I am so tired crying tears that feel like fire*
*I need You to pull me through*
*I have prayed, praised*
*Fasted and quoted scriptures*
*What else would You have me to do*
*I'm tired of smothering my screams*
*So that no one else will hear*
*I water seeds of promise…*
*With my own sweat and tears*
*I'm hurting in a place that only You see*
*I wear an air-brushed smile on my face*
*But in my heart there's a pain so deep*
*Still I'm fighting the good fight of faith*
*If I don't tell nobody the truth…*
*Lord I have to tell it to You…*
*And the truth is…*
*I don't feel like fighting today*
*I am disappointed, discouraged*
*Tired, embarrassed*
*I can be myself with You*
*Never do I have to be the great pretender…*
*What I want right now…is to throw in the towel…*
*But I don't even have white flag to wave in surrender*
*I wanna handle every situation in a way that makes You proud*
*Through the mess and the madness, I listen for Your voice…*
*But God the distractions are loud*
*I'm wrestlin' demons*
*Fightin' failure*
*Fallin' as I run this race*
*I feel like everybody's pointin', & laughin'*
*Even the rain feels like spit in my face*

*My palms are bleedin'*
*From grippin' tight to my faith*
*And I don't know any more prayers to pray*
*I don't know what scriptures to read…*
*All I know is long ago*
*You gave me a promise to believe*
*I want You to tell the Moses in my life*
*To stretch forth his rod and part the sea*
*I want You to let me through on dry ground*
*And swallow every enemy that comes after me*
*Lord my life is a catastrophe*
*I'm so tired of battling*
*I've been pushed beyond my limits*
*Beaten beyond recognition*
*But I will not curse You and die*
*You're all I have*
*All I really know*
*You are God and not a man that You should lie*
*Father, I feel like the pressure that's on me*
*Is so much more than I can stand*
*This time, my mamma or my husband can't help*
*What I need done…*
*Only You can*
*I look to Thee for help Dear God…*
*I know that You'll see me through*
*Be it only the size of a mustard seed…*
*My faith abounds in You*

## THIRSTY

My throat is dry
My heart is heavy…
My face is damp with tears
My head is tight
I squint my eyes…waitin' on change to appear
I feel like I'm drownin' in the pressures of life
Can't hold my breath no longer
Be anxious for nothing
The Bible warns
Yet, my anxiety grows stronger and stronger
All I want is everything
Joy, health, love, prosperity and peace
I want all of hell's devils and every bill collector
At once to stop chasin' me
Cuz I can't run no faster
I can't fight no harder
I can't scream no louder
God why should I bother
I read Your word…and the promises therein
Faithful Father, All Knowing Creator
He who called me friend
Then…
Tell me why do I continue to cry
Why do tears of vinegar
The color of blood
Constantly sting my eyes
Why does my hair lose it's thickness
Exposing the shame and pain of my bare scalp
Why am I rocked to sleep by demons
Unable to unconsciously relax
God is this the purpose for which I was created
Was I made to suffer defeat
I love You even if this is my plight…
But Lord have mercy on me
What is it…

*Have I done something to upset You*
*Have I been disobedient and wrong*
*God tell if I've offended Thee*
*I'm repenting please...*
*Forgive me for all that I've done*
*My soul is dry and thirsty*
*The air is too thick to breathe*
*Either bring me deliverance*
*Or bring me a Word*
*That You desire not to deliver me*
*But Lord I ask that You give me a sign*
*Father, I call on Your Name*
*I don't mean to be perverse or unbelieving*
*But God my soul is in pain*
*I've done everything that I can do*
*I've taken as much as I can take*
*God said...*
*If you believe My Word*
*Then you know that it says*
*You too must suffer for My sake*
*Don't you know that I am right there with you*
*Not once have I left your side*
*It is My shoulder that you lean against*
*Every time you cry*
*Never have I left you*
*Never will I forsake you...*
*Not for a second will I do it..*
*I know that the road you travel is tough...*
*But I'm the One who's carrying you through it*
*Don't you know I know all things*
*Don't you believe I care*
*The things you go through are only to strengthen you*
*I'll never give you more than you can bare*
*I know the burden is heavy for you*
*I know it's hard to hold*
*But if you peek around every obstacle...*
*You'll see that My Hand has never let go*
*I know of your physical changes*

41

*Even those you don't understand*
*I watch you close…*
*Whether hair falls, or grows…*
*I have not lost count of one single strand*
*The reason the demons chase you to sleep*
*As often as it seems*
*Is only because as much as you say…*
*You haven't given Me everything*
*Some things you've relinquished*
*But some things, you still hold*
*Tell Me, what is that you can do without Me…*
*What's beyond my control*
*Frustration comes, when you're not focused on Me*
*So I know that you're thirsty and dry*
*If you desire to be quenched by freedom*
*And drenched in blessings…*
*Know that I Am the Fountain of Life*
*Drink from Me liberally*
*That every void be filled…*
*Until it overflows*
*My Son is your light, your spirit the soil*
*It's My Word that Waters your soul*
*If you're dry and thirsty*
*And there is no harvest…*
*It's because you…*
*Don't want to grow*

# Chapter 2:
# Tears

*I have cried many tears for many reasons. These "tears" are special because they were shed over my children. Although I didn't cry while I was in labor, I have not ceased to cry since they have been born. Tears fall from pride, frustration, correction, concern, laughter, love and sheer amazement.*

*They that sow in tears shall reap in joy. (Psalm 126:5)*

## VICTORY FAITH

*I asked God to give me a little girl*
*In fact I requested His best*
*I wanted her to be beautiful indeed…*
*A perfect little princess*
*I prayed and waited, and waited and prayed*
*Still my womb was bare*
*God took His time, for you are a special design*
*From your feet, right up to your hair*
*I get lost starring into your beautiful eyes*
*And find myself looking at your pretty face*
*In a dream God told me what I should call you…*
*That's why I named you Victory Faith*
*Take your place in my heart…*
*No one ever could*
*Now I know what took so long…*
*God was making you extra good*
*I call you Inka-Binka*
*My bouncin' baby girl*
*Who knew that little bitty you*
*Could be the center of my great big world*

*Hugs & Kisses,*
*Mommy*

# A CHILD

*A child is like a blank canvas*
*Already wonderful, but the potential to become so much more*
*Waiting to explore, dream, decide, to change*
*To live like never before*
*A child's mind is the painter's pallet*
*Holding different shades, tones, & hues*
*Give children brushes, & let them create*
*You'd be surprised at what they can do*
*So I give to you, my children...*
*Sunshine's yellow, fire engine reds, midnight sky blues*
*Glittering gold, & summer grass green*
*And the freedom you need to choose*
*I grant you the ability to paint your own canvas*
*Reaching out from inside yourself*
*May your life be a work of art on the Creator's wall*
*To be enjoyed by everyone else*
*There are no borders, no thick black lines*
*Decorate your tomorrows...*
*By what you see today in your mind*
*And if what you made isn't what you wanted it to be*
*At the time that you began*
*God will erase all your mistakes, and allow you to start again*
*Find the strength in your heart to do what you love*
*And always love what you do*
*Make the art exhibit of life even more beautiful*
*With the courage to create a portrait of you*

## MIRACLES

*I believe in God whom I've never seen*
*I've skipped stones across the ocean*
*And danced on moon beams*
*I've been blessed with the best that Heaven can give*
*I have the chance to love while I live*
*I have seen miracles that are so far beyond my view*
*I may have never known love if I never had you*
*A blessing waiting on the verge of my destruction, you are*
*Don't know if I ever told you...*
*But you're the center of my heart*
*It was your tears that pushed me*
*When I could go no further*
*When I had no more to give*
*Your smile reminded me why I live*
*At my weakest points*
*I found strength in you*
*Love is the force behind all I do*
*I may have never tasted life*
*Had it not been for your flavor*
*Somehow I'll find a way to return the favor*
*In tears I'm simply speechless at the thought of you*
*Like a genie in a lamp*
*You're too good to be true*
*Never an accident...*
*A necessary happening*
*Cuz' I know...*
*If the devil would have had his wish...*
*I would have erased my existence and missed all this*
*Through moments of frustration*
*I'm screaming to the sky*
*God sent rain to wash the tears from my eyes*
*For me, wind isn't wind at all...*
*It's the breath from a sweetly blown kiss*
*A reminder that miracles and the Maker of them all*
*Without a doubt exist...*

*Unforgettable is your kiss*
*And the touch of your hand*
*You make simple, the things that are hard to understand*
*Honestly, at hello…*
*You captured me like a wish in the breeze…*
*And for me… it was awesome*
*I was no more than the bud of a rose…*
*It was you who helped me blossom*
*You held me in the span of time*
*I couldn't escape your grasp…*
*Because of you, I can push through pain*
*There's energy in your laugh*
*You are unscripted, unrehearsed*
*Exploring each other*
*Is like traveling the universe*
*Time becomes irrelevant*
*There's no difference between*
*Now, then or later*
*I fell asleep in the middle of the planet*
*In your arms I woke up on the edge of the equator*
*Still covered by your kisses like a blanket of stars*
*Somehow you figured out how to remove all the scars*
*You amaze me…*
*Mine was said to be a barren womb…*
*God allowed you only to give me babies*
*And I'm grateful*
*Because I know…*
*If the devil would have had his wish*
*I would have erased my existence*
*And missed all this*
*And those eyes…*
*They outshine the stars in the sky*
*I met you in a dream*
*A beauty such as yours…*
*I've never before seen*
*Stronger and more delicate than I'll ever be*
*Like platinum snowflakes*
*And butterfly wings*

*Your spirit is pure*
*And your soul is sweet*
*You slipped thru the fingertips of despair*
*There is honor in your heart*
*And glory in your hair*
*Eyelashes that stretch*
*The length of a mile*
*The warmest ray of sunshine*
*Is trapped in your smile*
*God allowed man to name every creature, himself*
*But your name He whispered with His own breath*
*And for me…*
*Wind isn't wind at all…*
*It's the breath from a sweetly blown kiss*
*A reminder that miracles and the Maker of them all*
*Without a doubt exist…*

# DRAELON

*I carried you in my womb*
*Worried, and confused*
*Will I be a good mommy to my baby*
*I was only a girl and my entire world*
*Changed instantly…and I cried*
*Nine months later…*
*You arrived, my pride and joy*
*The doctor said…*
*Mommy, you have a baby boy*
*Bundled in blankets I brought you home*
*A piece of heaven for my very own*
*I dressed you, and rocked you, and feed you, and read to you*
*You learned how to pull yourself up and eat with a spoon*
*Before I could wake up*
*You had already crawled out of my room*
*I heard you giggling, happy as can be*
*Grandma feed you breakfast, while you sat on Grandpa's knee*
*You were so little then, and I couldn't wait for you to walk and talk*
*Before I knew it…*
*You were runnin' and rappin'*
*Sayin' "what's up" to lil' girls and askin' them "what's happenin' "*
*I saw you grow right before my eyes*
*And I cried*
*I use to pick out your clothes, and make you look so cute*
*The cute clothes were replaced by "raw" fits*
*And now you only want a certain kind of shoe*
*I watched you out the window playin' rough, and scrubbin' up your knees*
*I gave you popsicles…*
*And told you not to go too far*
*Soon, I'll be giving you my keys and tellin' you to be careful with my car*
*As I slowly watch you grow*
*I slowly let you go*
*And I pray that God will forever guard your heart*
*I get butterflies thinking about your graduation day*
*I'll be so proud watching you walk across that stage*

I never thought of you as an accident
But a surprise that became the center of my life
Of all the little girls you'll smile at...
One will become your wife
And I won't get all the hearts you drew for me
Or the love notes filled with sweet words
Cuz' she'll take my place, and be the best girl in the world
And everything that you gave to me...
You'll give to her
Of the millions of wrong things that I've done in my life
I watch you sleep, and kiss your cheek
And I know I did one thing right
I ask God to put extra hours in our days
I need more time, Lord please understand
I blinked my eye less than a second...
And my little boy is becoming a young man
Drae, I want you to know
That when you get old...
When your face is wrinkled, and your hair is gray
Many, many years from now
I'll blow a cool breeze your way
That will carry my kisses
As I watch you from Heaven's clouds

# BECAUSE OF YOU

*Because of you*
*I got all emotional and couldn't stop crying...or eating*
*I couldn't fit the clothes that I just bought*
*To show off how much weight I lost*
*Cuz I ain't so small no more...*
*Everything that use to sit up...is heading towards the floor*
*Because of you*
*I don't own any midriffs*
*I'm not toned and tight*
*And my abs are not ripped...*
*At three AM, as I'm makin' a bottle*
*I realize...I'll never be a swim suit model*
*I'll never grace the pages of a magazine*
*Curves flowin' like water...*
*Slim and lean*
*Because of you*
*I don't have time for me, cuz' all my time is yours*
*I spend it hugging, teaching, correcting...*
*And reminding you of your chores*
*Because of you*
*I've had sleepless nights*
*Up praying about the pain of teething...*
*And preventing school fights*
*Because of you*
*I have had more reasons to talk to Jesus*
*I have more questions to ask*
*Like, "Father, am I doing this right?"*
*And, "How long will this thing last?"*
*Because of you*
*18 is just a number*
*You'll always be my babies...*
*And I'll always be your mother*
*I don't like everything you do*
*But no matter what you do...*
*I'll always love you*

*Because of you*
*I'll put my dreams on hold*
*To hold you…*
*As I encourage you to live your dreams*
*Because of you*
*I've spanked and screamed*
*And sent you to your room*
*Only to go to mine in tears*
*Cuz it's hard chastising you*
*I have to train you up in the way that you should go*
*If I don't teach you right from wrong…*
*How else are you gonna know*
*Because of you*
*I've learned the value of a home-cooked meal*
*A dollar, a dime, and time*
*I've learned to fold clothes, wipe noses*
*Burp one baby, and tell the other to say "excuse me" when he burps…*
*All at the same time*
*I've learned that my 9 to 5 is a means to survive*
*Being a mommy is the real work*
*Because of you*
*I'm heavy with guilt and shame…*
*This season I missed every one of your basketball games*
*I missed the banquet, sorry I didn't see you get your trophy*
*I know I'm always busy…*
*It seems I'm constantly working…*
*To plant seeds for a prosperous future…*
*And I do it*
*Because of you…*
*Because of you*
*I'm paranoid that I'll miss your first steps*
*I'm prying pennies out of your mouth*
*And always smelling your breath*
*To make sure you didn't eat something you weren't suppose to*
*I've been puked on, pooped on, peed on, sneezed on*
*All because of you*
*I've learned that there is a delicate balance between mother and friend*
*You need to know that I am both*

*Without mixing up which takes precedence over the other*
*We can laugh one minute, and I'll smack you the next...*
*Remember, I am your mother*
*Because of you*
*I have inherited..."the look"*
*The gift of communication, without the use of words*
*It tells you that I've had as much as I can take*
*And you're gettin' on my nerves*
*Because of you*
*I grit my teeth and answer questions about sex that I wish you wouldn't ask*
*But I'd rather you ask me...*
*Then learn in the street*
*Because of you*
*I view teenage girls as a personal threat*
*Little bitty tempters and liars*
*Sent to tear down my empire*
*Because of you*
*I now understand my mother-in-law...*
*It's wasn't me that she didn't like...*
*She just loved your daddy more than life*
*I know you gotta have girlfriends before you have a wife*
*You better be selective, she better be respectful*
*Use your spiritual eyes to see*
*Because of you*
*I want her to be better than me*
*Because of you*
*I have to be the perfect lady*
*I know you're watchin' though you're still a baby*
*You're lookin' and learnin...*
*So I can't be slippin'*
*You need to see me prayin' and fastin'*
*Instead of fussin' and trippin'*
*Because of you*
*I'll have to remember all the tricks I pulled*
*Stay five steps ahead of you...*
*To cut out all the bull*
*Check your book bag at the door*

*Take out the perfume…*
*And the lip gloss with color*
*I don't have x-ray vision…*
*But I was a girl, before I was your mother*
*Because of you*
*I'll teach you the importance of self respect*
*I'll tell you that your body is a sanctuary…*
*Not a playground*
*For just anybody to get*
*But it is for your husband alone…*
*Because of you*
*I'll have to face the day you walk away…*
*As you go, know you can always come back home*
*Because of you*
*I've learned how to love and how to give*
*Now I know what has value, and what is worthless…*
*I thank God for you daily…*
*Because of you…*
*My life has purpose*


*"I am so honored that God chose me to birth angels"*

# Chapter 3:
# Trials

*Trials is a bittersweet aroma. It has been said that the things that don't kill us, make us stronger. I don't know if that's completely true. I can attest to the fact that life's difficult times builds character in the one who endures. Failed relationships, bad decisions, disappointments, and heart wrenching pain are a part of life. They are necessary to make us grow, to make us better...to make us shine. Nothing great has ever been accomplished without a trial. Gold isn't beautiful before the fire, and a diamond without pressure is just a piece of coal. I have learned, and am yet learning that a test is the prelude to a testimony. Embrace every part of life, and thank the Lord for it all...*

*How that in a great trial of affliction the abundance of their joy and their deep poverty abounded unto the riches of their liberality.(2 Corinthians 8:2)*

## EMOTIONAL RELAPSE

I wanna have an emotional relapse
And relax
Go way back...
At least six months ago when we first tasted love
First savored the sweet honey that covered each other's lips
Or licked liquid love drops that dripped from each other's hips
I wanna be that thing that satisfies your sweet tooth
In a world of lies, I want you to share my truth
I want you
Even more than I use to
I don't know what's worse...
Leaving me alone, or leaving me confused
I just want to lay next to you
Cuz you're special
Loving you was natural and simple
What felt easy, feels quizzical
What felt real, feels mythical
Fictional even
Still, I'm believin'
That dreams really do come true
I fell asleep wishin' on stars...
Woke up to me and you
And we experienced love like no other
You can't say we didn't
We can deny every tear we cried...
But who are we kiddin'
Three months away from a wedding day that was prophesied by angels
Signed by God, and written in the stars
Now because of past love that was tainted
Wishes that were twisted
We fear what's rightfully ours
I already got too many scars
Too many broken hearts
Too many regrets
Too many memories, I wish I could forget

*I don't understand*
*If I give you my heart, and place forever in the palm of your hand…*
*What more do I owe you*
*How else can I show you*
*The actions of words, it seems that you refuse to believe*
*I should be making plans to spend forever with you*
*Instead of dreading the day you decide to leave*
*Are you having a change of heart*
*Or is this just cold feet*
*It's me, who'll massage your feet*
*And warm your cold, and cool your hot*
*It's me who makes we*
*And you who makes us*
*And love is all we've got*
*And if I'm love to you…*
*Then what are you afraid of*
*We made history, when we made love*
*We made the present much more gifted*
*With kisses we lifted the future out of tomorrows existence*
*And placed it in a time called…right this instant*
*We choked the very breath that God breathed in you and me*
*We removed faith, and put doubt in it's place*
*We replaced hope with fear*
*Now, we're uncertain of what was our surety for the past year*
*You keep me guessin', constantly testin'*
*Questioning…are we moving too fast*
*You're decorating our future, with the remains of your past*
*I'll be ok if you look at me today*
*And say you don't know if I'm your wife*
*If you can't trust in what we call love*
*Then just trust in the love of Christ*
*Put none of your faith in me*
*Put it all in God above*
*Cuz right now I'm having an*
*Emotional relapse, I just wanna relax*
*And go way back*
*To the moment we first tasted love*

# LIFE DON'T LISTEN

I never asked to be conceived
Only to grieve the loss of a father
Who isn't even deceased
Still the daily pollutants I breathe
Slowly kill my brain cells causing me to be
At ease
At a time that isn't even easy
Visibly black
With invisible chains...
Still waiting for somebody to free me
Just think me free, how different life would be
Now the concept of freedom itself is a trip
Still ticked cuz my great-great granny was shackled on a ship
And stripped of her identity, and of her innocence
Kidnapped, slave-trapped and re-named Jemison
And now you mad
Cuz I won't recite the pledge we rehearsed
I'm not disrespecting your flag...
Just payin' homage to mine first
Ain't never done you no wrong
Still you can't stand me
Got me feelin' like the black Annie
Adopted by a country that aborts my kind
As a means of stopping crime
My mind is heavy with the weight of stressful issues
I've cried more tears than I can count
Kleenex can't make enough tissues
To dry my over-flowing eyes
I don't count sheep to get to sleep
I pray and I cry
Cuz my sky...
My sky to black to see stars
So, I just stopped wishin'
Makin' all requests known to God...
Cuz life itself don't listen

*I was cursed at birth*
*Sayin' my time on earth*
*Was nuthin' but an impossible mission*
*And what's twisted...*
*It don't even matter that I'm young, ambitious, and gifted*
*I'm six shades too dark to be considered light...*
*So they labeled me a she-breed misfit*
*Just another statistic*
*And somebody told me that my body was a temple*
*That should have been simple*
*But I behaved sinful*
*And with one act it was defiled*
*In nine short months my stomach was pumped*
*Mamma held my hand as I gave birth to her first grandchild*
*He was beautiful ya'll, but still I couldn't smile*
*I was just a kid myself*
*Suddenly responsible for the life of someone else*
*Mamma said that I was still her little angel*
*And that I was heaven sent*
*I wanted to believe her*
*But the devil had my mind bent*
*As a kid, my innocence was stained crimson*
*He picked the lock on my magic box*
*And he should be in prison...but he isn't*
*And for years my screams echoed*
*And there was none ever helpful...*
*And now I know it's cuz life wasn't listenin'*
*But I listened...I listened when he told me*
*He loved me so much he'd put the ring on my left hand*
*Then he left*
*Gave that same love to someone else*
*And said he hoped I could understand*
*Man...*
*He did what he promised he'd never do*
*He left me all alone*
*Kissed me on the cheek*
*Told me to stay sweet*
*And reminded me that life goes on*

*And one morning, I'm up and gettin' ready for church*
*And I'm tellin' God He's the only one who can fix this hurt*
*As I raised my hands and gave Him praise it worked*
*And all of my voids were spiritually filled for real*
*And I don't think nobody is takin' this time seriously*
*And sometime I don't think nobody even think about it but me*
*But the earth is the devil's playground*
*He got us all spellbound*
*If we don't redirect our paths, no doubt*
*We'll be hell bound*
*Well now…this globe we call home*
*This here about to be blazin'*
*But because you ain't seen it*
*You don't believe it*
*And all ya'll think that I'm crazy*
*Amazin'*
*And I know you heard it before…*
*But the world is really endin'*
*Iniquity is surrounding me, and ain't nobody repentin'*
*Ignore the smile on my face*
*Cuz my inner man is mournin'*
*We livin' in the last days*
*The book of Revelation sends warning*
*And I'm running through the streets*
*Yellin' FIRE, tryin' to*
*Get your attention*
*The gates of Heaven are opened…*
*Jesus paid your admission*
*You nodded your head as you heard what I said*
*Then went right back to your old act*
*Cuz life itself don't listen*
*Loose-lipped, tongue slipped*
*I stutter confused*
*It's to the point I can't even watch the news…*
*Ain't no more apples ya'll*
*They passin' out condoms at school*
*And we got brothers killin' each over shoes*
*Just to prove who's who*

*And the mammas can't care for the babies*
*Cuz they chasin' the daddies in the streets*
*As I smell burned rubber*
*My thoughts are interrupted*
*By the tires that screech*
*Outside...house down the block*
*Just shot up from a drive by*
*And for the first time in a long time*
*He cried,*
*As his girlfriend lay limp at his right side*
*The bullet meant for him...*
*Put her under the sheet*
*He kissed her stomach and said good-bye*
*To the baby he'll never see*
*Now days sixteen, ain't so sweet*
*And Monday morning when the school bell rang*
*J.R. wasn't in class*
*Fell victim to the chrome*
*Shot in the back of the dome*
*Left dead on his mamma's grass*
*The life we live tends to speed up*
*And go way, way too fast*
*Who woulda thought that yesterday would of been the future doctor's last*
*He spent 182 on the new tennis shoes*
*He'll never even wear*
*Cuz his toe is tagged*
*They snatched his last breath*
*And his Foot Locker bag*
*And what do we do*
*We turn our heads*
*Cuz the state of the world is sad*
*And though we hate to admit it*
*We're trapped in hatred and ignorance*
*Ignoring all positivity*
*Cuz life itself...*
*Don't listen*

# DADDY

*i gotta write you this letter*
*cuz i got some questions that i need the answers to*
*looking thru - old photos*
*i saw no pictures of me and you*
*i don't have many memories of Christmas gone past*
*there were no family trips, a few birthday gifts*
*way more tears than laughs*
*see, there are so many things i wanna ask*
*but i can't even talk to you*
*don't know how to approach you*
*half of my genetic make up is yours...*
*and i don't even know you*
*there are parts of me you ain't even seen*
*cuz i'm too scared to show you*
*i don't want you to be disappointed at the way i turned out*
*there's a little girl trapped inside of me,*
*and she's crying and screaming out*
*and she wants you to hug her and tell her everything is ok*
*i keep trying to make her realize that part of her life has gone away*
*time is unforgiving, it's gone, it's too late*
*tears fill my eyes as i realize*
*i'm in a great debate*
*with me*
*i'm fightin' with myself...*
*i don't wanna be your mistake, or your forgotten*
*a burden given to someone else*
*i just want to be your daughter*
*what ever that means*
*i want you to look at me and remember the moment of my birth*
*i want you to see me and think that i'm the best thing on earth*
*i want you to buy me ice cream, and take me to the movies*
*doesn't have to be just you and me*
*i don't mind if my sisters and brother come*
*i just wanna feel like one of your children*
*not the only one*

*as for child support and explanations…*
*you don't owe me none*
*i've been trying to escape these feelings…*
*for my whole life i've tried*
*but it's kind of hard when i look in the mirror*
*and i'm being stared at by your eyes*
*if any of it was my fault…i apologize*
*i would like to know if it was something that i did*
*what on earth would make you leave your kid*
*did i cry too much, did i kick and scream,*
*was i too loud, did i disturb your sleep*
*i got these tears streaming from my eyes that can't nobody else wipe away*
*i wish you wouldn't of missed my graduation day*
*i know i had my son when i was in the eleventh grade…*
*but daddy… i made it, i had a baby on my hip, but i still graduated*
*i didn't finish, but i did go to college*
*i majored in psychology, with a business minor*
*i've always been a writer…*
*but i was goin' for my PhD*
*i thought maybe if i became a doctor…you'd be proud of me*
*daddy, why don't you like me, do i remind you of my mother*
*she couldn't have been that bad*
*after all…you are my dad*
*or is that the fact in which you are in denial*
*did you slip up…and i came out lookin' just like you*
*i never denied you…never even tried to*
*i was so proud to say, my daddy is from Jamaica*
*then they'd ask me what part*
*i'd get a lump in my throat, and a pain in my heart…*
*cuz i don't even know*
*there's so much i wanna know*
*i'm grown*
*with a husband and children of my own*
*and part of me still…*
*wants my daddy*
*how badly i wish i had you*
*dad you*
*are my missing piece*

*i'm in my husbands arms fast asleep*
*and still i reach… for you*
*i just wanna hold your hand*
*and maybe your attention, just for a moment or two*
*you never told me i was beautiful*
*i never got to run to you*
*i won't ask you to explain your absence*
*it doesn't really matter what happened*
*i never got a chance to draw you a picture*
*no refrigerator art to display*
*but i do write poems and put them in frames*
*if you wanna see…i'll make you one someday*
*i'm extending my hand to you*
*i just want a chance to*
*know you*
*i know you're busy with life and all*
*but if you ever get a minute…could you give me a call*
*i mean…you got a grand daughter that you've never even seen*
*if you want me too, i'll come to you*
*we haven't seen each other in years*
*and you live right up the street*
*i don't want to push myself on you…*
*if you still don't want me, it's ok*
*no matter what, i'll still pray…for you*
*i can't lie your absence left a wound*
*in my soul*
*i try to look at it from your perspective…*
*maybe you just didn't know*
*what to do, or how to be a father*
*don't even bother with that then*
*can we start over, and maybe just be friends*
*thinkin' back you know what comes to mind…*
*you said if i needed anything, to call you*
*you dropped off money, but i wanted time*
*i wanted you to really care for me*
*i just wanted you to be there for me*
*wanna hear something crazy*
*in the third grade, i was in a spelling bee*

*and i kept imagining that you would slip through the back door*
*you would give me a thumbs up, and be my source of support*
*you never made it...but it's ok*
*i couldn't spell scissors anyway...*
*have to think hard to spell that word to this day*
*every memory i have ain't sad...i'm not sayin' you were all bad*
*i'm just simply statin' the facts, in fact*
*i must have been about ten*
*i remember when*
*you took us to a parade*
*i had so much fun that day...just cuz i was with you*
*dad i miss you*
*and i wanted you know, that the past is the past*
*you'll always be my dad*
*and i'll always love you so*
*i know*
*that i am my husband's queen*
*i just hate the fact that i never got to be...*
*your princess*
*so much for regrets*
*i just*
*wanted you to know*
*you can never really leave a child*
*in your absence*
*they'll still grow*
*being created into something the whole while*
*boys transform into toy soldiers...*
*and girls like me...*
*broken dolls*

## WALK PAST ME

*As he kissed my lips*
*My hips shifted*
*Giving him permission*
*To complete his mission*
*Which is impossible*
*If his obstacle*
*Is to gain access to my heart*
*Cuz for too many years, I've cried too many tears*
*I've overcome too many fears…*
*To be right back here*
*Again*
*Where I wade through waters too deep to swim*
*Not enough time has passed for me to be so into him*
*He's so attentive to me*
*He's everything that I need him to be*
*Without me, ever having to ask*
*He makes me laugh*
*Like the first time the blind*
*Beheld the sunrise*
*I had an inner battle, just to keep the tears from falling from my eyes*
*Cuz I don't think he'd understand why I'd cry*
*So I pushed that emotion to the back of my mind*
*I pushed it so far back that it traveled to a previous time*
*When I first realized*
*The thing that hurts the worst*
*Is what started out feeling the best*
*I feel his breath on my neck*
*And I let my head rest…*
*Upon his shoulder*
*When I was younger*
*I looked forward to the wisdom that would come when I got older*
*Now that older is here*
*I realize, I'm as dumb as I was when I was young*
*Cuz here I am again*
*Trying to win a battle*

That I feel I'm destined to lose
I feel as if I'm backed in a corner
Forced to choose
The permanent peace of being alone
Or, temporary happiness with you
We converse through touch
So much to say
I'm trying to tell you that I'm afraid
I'm paralyzed by the fear of the inevitable…
I want you to walk away
I know you won't stay
When you see the baggage I'm left with
From guilt trips
You're strong…
But this is too much for you to carry
My heart is heavy
So because I like you
I'd like to invite you
To walk past me, and not look back
Cuz I attract…
Pain
And I don't want my acid
To rain
Upon your head
You're special, and I can't let you
Get entangled in danger
And resentment
Pretending it is, what it isn't
Since the moment my womb became my son's home
My life hasn't been my own
I'm not even at leisure to fall in love when I'd like
Cuz everything I do…
Affects his life
Sound crazy…it might
But for the next eight years I'll sacrifice
Playing house
So that he can have a stable home
His father left and forgot come home

*And now his stepfather is gone*
*I gotta be careful about what he sees*
*I can't let him look at you…*
*And see daddy number three*
*And I can't stop these tears from falling*
*As I think about your touch*
*And how good you make me feel*
*Could this possibly be real*
*For me…*
*Will anything ever be*
*How much time will pass before you tell me you love me*
*And you need me*
*How much more time will pass before you make love to me*
*Then leave me*
*How long will it be before you no longer have time*
*To drive all the way to my house*
*Just to kiss me good night*
*How long before we stop fighting passion*
*And just start to fight*
*When exactly will insults take the seat*
*Where compliments use to sit*
*In your eyes I'm no longer beautiful…*
*Just another wench*
*And the sweetness of the lips that you once loved to kiss*
*Will become bitter to your taste*
*Today you love looking at me*
*But tomorrow, you won't wanna see my face*
*As I write this from my special place*
*I can still smell your scent*
*Maybe my wisdom is kicking in*
*Cuz I've learned from my past mistakes*
*Failed relationships, and broken hearts*
*Sometimes your fiction…*
*Is my fact*
*So because I like you*
*I'd like to invite you*
*To walk past me and not look back*

## ONE LAST POEM

*If I were to write you one last poem…*
*I wouldn't waste paper or ink, asking*
*What went wrong*
*I'd ask that you'd listen to the wind and hear love songs*
*But not the depressing ones that make you*
*Wish you could forget me*
*But the one that says…*
*Even though it didn't work out*
*You're still so glad you met me*
*I would ask that sometimes when you think of me*
*You'll smile as a tear traces the curve of your cheek*
*Miss me, but feel close like you would*
*A friend who left this world too soon*
*Taste my tears when it rains*
*See my face in the moon*
*Do this as you remember me…*
*Because I do them, as I remember you*
*The time we've been apart*
*Will never match the time we spent together*
*Some nights I still lose sleep*
*I wish I could hate you to heal this hurt*
*But I can't, because I loved you too deep*
*You were supposed to be one with me*
*And I with you…*
*We promised each other forever*
*When we said "I do"*
*Not enough nights were spent praying*
*Too many nights spent away from home*
*Staying…*
*Everywhere, except where we needed to be*
*I should have been there for you*
*You should have been there for me*
*Too many misunderstandings*
*Life got too demanding*
*Time was unforgiving*

*Pain wasn't worth reliving*
*I'm left feeling awkward*
*Cuz, I can't call you lover*
*And I can't call you friend*
*I can't call you at all*
*Because of how we had to end*
*If I had to do it all over again*
*I would have never given you my number to call*
*Who said it was better to have loved and lost*
*Than to have never loved at all*
*If I would have never loved you*
*This pain wouldn't be mine to bear*
*My heart wouldn't be crushed at all*
*If at first I never cared*
*Most of all*
*I wouldn't recall...*
*Promising each other, we'd always be there*
*Our words rip through each other*
*Anger cuts like the blade of a knife*
*If I were brave enough to be honest with you*
*I'd tell you that you fulfilled my heart's desire*
*The day you took me to be your wife*
*So why am I running so fast towards leaving...*
*Because in our love, you stopped believing*
*I don't wanna hurt no more*
*I don't wanna cry*
*I don't wanna leave...*
*But I gotta say good-bye*

# TONIGHT I WATCHED YOU SLEEP

*Tonight I watched you sleep*
*I let my eyes fall all over you the way my words do*
*Whenever I begin to speak about you*
*Tonight I watched you sleep and a small part of me*
*Wanted to crawl into your arms and cry*
*I refrained from letting my soul's rain fall from my eyes*
*Splash on your chest and form puddles of spilled emotion*
*Sometimes when I feel like this I just want to sleep…*
*Don't want to write a poem about it*
*Don't wanna have to think about words that rhyme*
*Or where to begin and end a line*
*Just want to write fast*
*Fast enough to release what ever anger and anguish*
*And fear and resentment*
*That's trapped inside of me*
*I don't wanna even worry about capitalization, and punctuation*
*Or correct spelling*
*Not giving a damn if I cross my t's or dot my i's*
*Just keep writing to expose the lies*
*That were passed off as truth to me so long ago*
*I just want to write and keep writing*
*Until this emptiness in the pit of my stomach is filled and I can no longer hear…*
*The echo of bad decisions in my head*
*I'm scared…*
*That if I don't keep writing then I'll start thinking too hard*
*And begin to tell myself how I feel*
*Instead of really feeling myself*
*I just want to want to be free*
*Whatever it is…*
*Where ever it is*
*I feel like there's so much about me that I don't even know*
*Yet I expect you to know how to make me happy*
*When I can't even do it for myself*
*I'm so scared of so many things*

*And tonight I wish I could crawl into you arms*
*Get right in your lap and cry*
*And let the tears burn my eyes*
*The way they've burned my heart*
*But I can't cuz…*
*You're sleeping*
*And I don't want to disturb you*
*I have so much baggage from the past it's hard for me to*
*Move forward*
*Sometimes I feel like I expect too much from you*
*I want you to make it all better*
*When I don't even know what's all wrong*
*I'm sorry for only being half sane*
*You know what…*
*I thought that if I lost weight, I'd be just fine*
*Sixty-five pounds lighter and I realize…*
*It was all in my mind*
*Don't get me wrong*
*I like the petite-ness of my frame*
*Still, I find myself feeling the shame*
*That put blisters on the soles of my feet*
*From running frantically from what ever reality*
*I have, that I don't wanna face*
*I wish I could tell you more, but honestly that's all I know*
*Can I tell you something that ran across my mind*
*Down my spine, and got stuck in my chest*
*Sometimes I feel like my best…*
*Isn't even good enough for you*
*No matter what I say or do, how well I cook or clean*
*I'll never measure up to the girl of your dreams*
*Or that girl in your past*
*Maybe I'm being silly, but I feel like*
*You look for things to complain about*
*My butt ain't big enough*
*My breast have started to sag*
*I lost all that weight*
*Now I got all this flab*
*I gotta laugh*

*Cuz' years ago I made a mental note in the margin of hope*
*As you said something about me being the perfect size six*
*At two hundred plus pounds and a size eighteen…*
*I felt like a six was unimaginable*
*Well, I'm a size eight*
*And you still got negative things to say*
*I try so hard to please you*
*When truthfully, sometimes I wish I didn't care*
*What you, or the rest of the world thought about me*
*I just want to take my flabby skin, saggy boobs, and flat behind*
*And go somewhere and celebrate Tisha…*
*As soon as I figure out exactly who she is*
*At least I'd like to spend some time trying to figure out…*
*What I really like*
*I wish I didn't need to hear you tell me that I'm beautiful*
*I wish I could look in the mirror and tell myself*
*So I think I'll stop wishing, and start doing*
*Tomorrow, when I wake…*
*I'll get up and wash my face*
*I'll greet my Father first…*
*Then I'll say "Good morning beautiful"*
*While looking in the mirror*
*It's funny how you think I have so much confidence*
*When the truth is…*
*I'm still pretending to have it all together*
*I want to be beautiful with my imperfections and all*
*I wish you could look at me and see…*
*Perfect imperfection, and absolutely love it*
*Have you ever noticed*
*I don't take time to point out what you need to improve*
*I'd rather spend that time focusing on your positive attributes*
*I wish you could do that for me*
*Some nights like tonight*
*I cry, pray, and write*
*Trying to find the point of it all*
*As I watch you sleep*

## BOTTOM LINE

*The bottom line is just what it is…*
*The bottom line*
*The final straw*
*I finally saw*
*The light*
*It explained all my hurt*
*As it exposed all your dirt*
*But I promised myself I'd be alright*
*Promised myself I'd stay strong*
*Promised myself I'd somehow be righted*
*For every one of your wrongs*
*What's wrong…*
*Why are you cryin'*
*Are you sick of lyin'*
*I'm sick of tryin'*
*Now you're in it to win it*
*But what you started*
*I'm ready to finish*
*Cuz' I'm fresh outta patience*
*Understanding, chances, and time*
*You can't even call for help…*
*Cuz' you dropped your dime*
*As I rolled away with tears in my eyes*
*I realized, you had me so low*
*I had to reach up to grab hold to…*
*The bottom line*

# I'M SORRY

*He broke my nose, and all his promises*
*He dislocated my jaw and cracked my ribs*
*I had his kids*
*I went out, he had a fit*
*He slapped my face and called me a wench*
*I needed some space so he replaced*
*Hickies with a neck brace*
*For so long I dreamed of our honeymoon*
*But the only trips we take are to the emergency room*
*As he feeds my the script on what to say*
*True, he hit my face, but then he kissed my face…*
*And said he was sorry*
*He said he was sorry*
*He actually apologized*
*Then he wiped the tears that fell from my eyes*
*And men don't do that unless they really love you*
*What, your man never shoved you*
*Never cut you with words, then with a knife*
*He really is into me…*
*But like enemies*
*We fight*
*He said one day he gone make me his wife*
*Sometimes I set off his temper with the things I say*
*And cause him to react in a violent way*
*But it's gone get better*
*Cuz he told me*
*He said it won't always be like this*
*Then he gently kissed…*
*The black eye he gave me for my birthday*
*I don't expect ya'll to understand, but…*
*I wanted to leave in the worse way*
*But how do you leave love*
*Why must I bleed love*
*How long would it be love*
*Before I felt a man twice my size knock me to the floor*

*How long would I be around to promise my babies it would be ok*
*And how long could I stand to see the confusion in their face*
*As I explain…*
*"It won't happen no more"*
*As I recall, one day I went to the store*
*And some man held open the door, so that I could pass through*
*It felt so nice, I smiled and said "thank you"*
*He asked my name, and he reached for a pen*
*I'm flattered, really…but I already have a man*
*He took a card from his pocket and put it in mine*
*He ran a shelter for battered women, and gave me a number to a hotline*
*Said he knew my kind*
*He saw the make-up I applied*
*Although it covered the bruises…it did nothing for my swollen eye*
*He never mentioned the iron print branded on my thigh*
*I got that for not creasin' my man's jeans right*
*I'm wearing turtle necks in seventy degrees*
*And I ain't foolin' nobody but me*
*I pretend to be blind, but the rest of the world sees*
*And again he hits me*
*But this time it lasts longer*
*His temper boils hotter*
*The impact of his punch is stronger*
*I got dizzy, the room was spinning*
*And I couldn't catch my breath*
*At the same time I tasted my blood, his sweat, and death*
*I grunted as his size thirteen invaded my stomach*
*He stomped me*
*I heard my babies cryin'*
*I lost control of my bodily fluids, I felt like I was dyin'*
*I don't remember speaking, but I heard myself say "call the cops"*
*My daughter screamed, "mommy, mommy"*
*My son begged, "daddy stop"*
*I imagined his sad eyes as the police took him away*
*I knew this time I would leave him for good, sure enough…*
*I died the next day*
*Now, I'm speaking to you from beyond the grave*
*I smile as I remember the nights I secretly prayed*

*Not once did I ask God to have His way…I just asked Him to accept mine*
*Three months after they buried me, I was right there at his trial*
*Hopin' for hard time*
*They slapped the hand that last slapped me*
*And with that they set him free*
*Nobody saw me, but they all felt me cryin'*
*How could they not, when my tears ran from the ceilings to the floors*
*The sound of my bare feet splashing through puddles nobody could ignore…*
*But they all did*
*To add insult to injury, they gave him custody of our kids*
*You see, as a father…he has rights*
*But where were mine the nights he started the fights*
*And the cops took their time*
*Cuz to them, domestic violence isn't really a crime…it's the usual for us*
*They pat his back as they lock his cuffs*
*Now my mamma blames herself, cuz I saw all this growing up, and she never left*
*Never whispered a breath, never told nobody she needed help*
*I remember better days…he wasn't always like this*
*I died tryin' to fight this*
*Correct the wrongs and right this*
*Tears fall as I write this, cuz it didn't have to be*
*Maybe I shoulda called the hotline, or ran to a shelter*
*Or sat in the very last pew at the church up the street*
*Maybe I shoulda really called on Jesus, instead of calling the police*
*All my maybe I shouldas don't have to be your reality*
*As long as there's breath in your body*
*And blood in your veins*
*And a God in heaven*
*Things can change*
*I had a life of destiny*
*And I traded it for tragedy*
*I just don't want all my maybe I shouldas…*
*To become your reality*

# REMEMBER ME

*I have only one favor to ask of you*
*Remember me in all that you say and do*
*Remember the way I danced*
*And the songs I liked to sing*
*Remember how I could find joy and laughter in almost anything*
*Remember how my smile of sunshine*
*Dried your tears of rain*
*Remember how my warm hug*
*Could erase your hurt and pain*
*Please remember all these things*
*Each time you remember me*
*And know that I'm only as far as you ever want me to be*
*It's beautiful and peaceful this place that I roam*
*It's nothing like the earthly place*
*This is really home*
*This is not goodbye*
*So dry those falling tears*
*Just remember me as I was*
*And I'll see you when you get here*
*Remember me as you pass by...*
*As you are, so was I*
*This earth is only temporary*
*We'll live together forever in eternity*
*There's one more thing I'd like to say...*
*Life doesn't stop because you don't see my face*
*As you live your life, thank God for each day*
*He gives us more than we realize...*
*Yet we don't take time to pray*

# SHOOTING STAR

*Pursuing you as a friend is like chaff in the wind*
*I've spent my whole life chasing a dream*
*Hoping that I could say something to make you laugh*
*Hoping to get close enough to get your autograph...*
*You've always been a star to me*
*Perhaps that's why you've always been*
*So far out of my reach*
*If you never ask...it doesn't matter...*
*I'm telling you that all is forgiven*
*I love you...*
*Without you I would have never existed*
*Thank you for things that you did...*
*As well as the things you didn't*
*Maybe it's too late*
*To be what I hoped we would be*
*No longer will I think of you as my life's missing piece...*
*To me, you're a shooting star*
*Just beyond my reach*

# I THOUGHT ABOUT YOU

*I thought about you this morning*
*I couldn't remember your eyes or your smile or how you walk*
*I couldn't remember your laugh*
*Or how your voice sounds when you talk*
*I didn't remember feeling safe in your arms*
*I couldn't remember the shape of your lips*
*Or the flavor of your kiss*
*Still this morning I thought about you*
*I thought about how you were the manifestation of every lie ever told*
*Looking at you was like watching a blanket of bad dreams unfold*
*You presented yourself as a friend*
*All the time you were a foe*
*You left scratches on my heart and rips in my soul*
*I was broken when you found me*
*And I wanted to be whole*
*I was a fragment of a woman*
*I was discarded from my ex's deck of cards*
*No longer was I his queen of hearts*
*You heard my spirit cry and caught my falling tears*
*And used them all for your advantage*
*You used the ointment of soothing words as a bandage*
*Which inevitably left a sting worse than before*
*What degree of wickedness does your heart hold*
*You didn't know me well enough to hate me*
*You held the remains of a woman murdered by love*
*And you sought ways to cremate me*
*Your fingerprints have long since*
*Left my skin*
*Still they remain on the heart that you mishandled*
*Lord, heal me*
*I'm tired of hearing*
*The repetition of bad decisions*
*And inhaling the reeking stenches*
*Of the scents of sin for which*
*I've already repented*

*I realized that although I've asked for forgiveness*
*I have not yet forgiven myself*
*Nor have I forgiven you*
*For being the vinegar of forbidden fruit*
*No longer am I plagued by your residue*
*What I did was prayed for you*
*The chains that held me, were broken loose*
*And now I'm free*
*I'm free from the scorn, I'm free from the shame*
*If ever again I should think of you*
*I won't feel the torment of pain*
*I won't feel your sting, your bite, or your burn*
*You're no longer a threat…but a quenched flame*
*God smothered the blaze*
*And you are a lesson well learned*

# Chapter Four:
## Triumphs & Inspirations

*The ingredients of "Triumphs & Inspirations" are essential to life. It is important to acknowledge every accomplishment, no matter how small it seems. Never wait to be inspired. Always be the inspiration. What ever life throws your way...take a deep breath, and smile. There is a bright side in every situation; you just have to choose to see it.*

*Now thanks be to God who always leads us in triumph in Christ, and through us diffuses the fragrance of His knowledge in every place. ( 2 Corinthians 2:14)*

# LIVING FOR THE MOMENT

*Let's sing songs*
*Write Poems*
*Gaze at stars*
*And draw hearts*
*All day*
*Let's spend time like money*
*And let none of it go to waste*
*Let's not wish upon stars*
*But make the stars wish*
*Upon themselves*
*Hoping to be as brilliant*
*As we are*
*Let's use words as they were*
*To mend hearts and*
*End wars*
*Let love be the water that washes the shores*
*And not adversity*
*Let's not worry about*
*What's beyond our control*
*Let's play like children*
*Pretending to be grown*
*Taking thought only for today*
*Tomorrow is too far away*
*With too many worries of it's own*
*Let's sway to the music that plays in our spirits*
*Only in silence are you able to hear it*
*Let's listen to words that have never been said*
*Let's recite scriptures from the books of the Bible we read*
*Let's tap dance between raindrops*
*And hop scotch across puddles*
*Let's not let many hours pass*
*Before we say I love you*
*Let's step back and breathe*
*And find our peace*
*For the world's pace is fast*

*Let's appreciate everything we take for granted*
*Instead of crying…*
*Let's just laugh*
*And everything that doesn't matter…*
*Just leave it in the past*
*Think not too much of yourself…*
*This moment is all you have*

## ALL GOD CALLED YOU TO BE

*God has filled you with such priceless treasure*
*You are His jewel, His precious gem*
*With hands and heart lifted*
*You have surrendered unto Him*
*It is with song you give praise*
*You worship through your tears*
*Every whispered prayer, and those unspoken*
*He hears*
*He listens for your voice…*
*You are His melody*
*Walk by faith be not afraid*
*Follow where ever He leads*
*Pour yourself out before Him*
*That you may again be filled*
*Speak those things that are not as if they were…*
*For His promises are real*
*Walk in your purpose*
*Pursue your destiny…*
*Be bold and live your dreams*
*God said that from you…*
*He would withhold no good thing*
*Be overtaken by His goodness, even when you don't see*
*God is the Author and Finisher of our faith*
*You shall be all that God called you to be…*

# I AIN'T GONE CRY

*I ain't gone cry no more today*
*I'm gone let go, and let God*
*I said, I ain't gone cry come what may*
*With God, the impossible ain't even hard*
*I won't complain about the falling rain*
*I'll stand against the strongest winds that blow*
*Yeah, I'm stuck in dirt, and mud right now…*
*But how else would a flower grow*
*I ain't gone cry no more today…*
*I'm gone wipe my nose and dry my eyes*
*When you see me tomorrow*
*You would have never known*
*That yesterday I cried*
*I can not carry this whole big burden*
*So I'm gone lay it at HIS feet*
*I'm casting all my cares upon the Lord*
*For I know HE cares for me…*

# RAIN

*I want it to rain*
*I want it to rain like it never has before*
*I want storms of liquid healing to pour*
*And cleanse my sorrows*
*I want it to rain tonight*
*To water the seeds I can't see*
*Harvesting for me, a beautiful tomorrow*
*Tonight I want it to rain*
*And what I'd really like*
*Is for each drop to tell a different story of my life*
*And by the time it's through raining*
*You will know everything there is to know about me*
*I want you to look at my face*
*And see these tears that I can't explain*
*And know that I'm not really cryin'*
*Rather, it's a downpour of spiritual rain*
*As God reminds me of the covenant that He and I made*
*When He and I prayed*
*Through the low places*
*The dry places*
*The desert places*
*Every space and place in my life*
*Where I - just needed*
*A little bit of rain*

# IN SEARCH OF ME

*Words whispered on feathery wings*
*Brings peace to a heart that stings*
*And burns, and yearns for a truth*
*More than the same painted lies*
*Through painted lips, and tinted eyes*
*Words are slurred*
*And vision is blurred*
*And I walked through the valleys not seeing*
*Just believing*
*All is well*
*I'm reaching for Heaven*
*And running from hell*
*Not feeling much of anything*
*Not knowing why the caged bird sings*
*Trying to remember what it is that makes me*
*Who I am…*
*It seems as if I no longer can*
*Hear myself*
*I'm trapped in silence*
*I can't get by it*
*I'm blocked by the loudness of the quiet*
*And I'm tryin'*
*To talk myself off my own emotional ledge*
*Either, I'm on the edge*
*Of the end, or the brink of a new dawn*
*My expectations go just beyond*
*My own limitations*
*I have no more zest or zeal*
*I can't figure out what's fake or real*
*I'm sitting still*
*Waiting for answers to questions that I'm too afraid to ask*
*Tired of tryin' to be patient*
*When truthfully I eagerly anticipate my fate*
*As it states within the pages of the Bible*
*With all my might*

*I'm trying to*
*Find out who*
*I am?*

## UN-DEFINABLE

*You can characterize me*
*But you can't define me*
*I'll always be more than what you see*
*My strength and wisdom is resilient*
*I'm absolutely brilliant*
*I don't even have to try to be*
*All I gotta do is*
*Keep peace, and love, and breathe, and believe*
*I am who I am because of He*
*I am more than a conqueror because He said it*
*I can do all things…*
*In His Word, I read it*
*Though the vision tarry…wait to see it*
*If you only got a little faith*
*Keep on believin'*
*But don't believe them*
*When they tell you what you can't do*
*Sometimes to get to where you going to*
*It takes some goin' through*
*Just persevere*
*Fear not for God said that He's with you*
*Some fiery darts will be shot…*
*But every one will miss you*
*They'll tell you a lot of things…*
*But I'm tellin' you, don't you listen*
*If you let their words occupy your soul*
*You're assistin' with their mission*
*You see, they said I wasn't pretty*
*Never looking*
*At the beauty within*
*They were too preoccupied with the shape of my eyes*
*The texture of my hair and the color of my skin*
*They were fixed*
*Focused on the exterior*
*The fact that I'm black*

*And female on top of that*
*Made me inferior...*
*I think not*
*I uprooted the seeds of what I could never be...*
*And planted myself as a tree of possibility*
*The flowers of potential*
*Blossoming on each one of my leaves*
*Leaves me to believe*
*I can achieve any thing*
*I can think of many things*
*The Creator can do exceedingly abundantly above all that I*
*can ask or think*
*I think that means...*
*I'm destined for greatness*
*As for depression, doubt, and despair...*
*I escaped them*
*Every discouraging word spoken to me...*
*I kill it with kindness and laugh*
*Who can say what I can't have*
*My future is up to me*
*I won't forfeit my choice*
*I have a voice*
*I don't need permission to speak*
*Or, think, or love, or cry, or pray*
*I need only believe the promise made to me...*
*For I can have whatever I say.*

# BLACK IS BEAUTIFUL

*You heard that black is beautiful*
*Let me tell you why*
*Black is the color of the midnight sky*
*Black is the creative curiosity of a child*
*In all it's glory*
*It's a black woman's smile*
*Black is hot and sexy like silk and lace*
*It's warm and caring like a mother's grace*
*Black is milk and honey, creamy caramel, and mocha bliss*
*It's thick rich fudge, the sweetest molasses*
*The very essence of a chocolate kiss*
*Black is bold and loud*
*Yet it keeps to itself*
*Black is an independent survivor, and relies on no one else*
*Black is the love a woman gives a man*
*When she satisfies the crave of his sweet tooth*
*Black is calm and reserved, cool and un nerved*
*Yet it has a tendency to scream the truth*
*It's the portrait of the wind*
*And the color of a melody…*
*Black is rhythm and blues, and jazz and hip-hop*
*And always light on it's feet*
*As I describe black in all that it is…*
*There is nothing else I'd rather be*

## DREAM SEQUEL

Martin had a dream
That all men were created equal
Last night, I fell asleep and dreamt the sequel
The playground was a safe place
For our children to play
And Milwaukee streets were peaceful
Children grew up to be cops
Instead of gettin' beat up by cops
In this dream we heard freedom ring
And not gunshots
Imagine that...
The ring of freedom's chime
Instead of the ring of a forty five or a nine
As it claims the life...
Of another dreamer
But I have a dream that blacks and whites will look beyond
Black and white
And realize in Christ
We're sisters and brothers
And leave colors...to crayola
I have a dream that black children
Won't think that using proper English is a white thing
And parents will begin to teach the right thing
And get back to a time when
We made our children believe...
They could be absolutely anything
I have a dream that men would stop acting like boys and accept
The responsibility of being husbands, and fathers
Instead of feelin' like a family is an inconvenience and a bother
Which disturbs the daily flow
Of them kickin' it
I have a dream instead of building more jails
The government would build more schools
And in the palm of a man's hand
Place the proper tools

*To allow him to be the architect who...*
*Builds his dreams*
*I have a dream that instead of teaching our kids to practice safe sex*
*We forbid them to have sex*
*Until their wedding day*
*I'm not getting carried away...*
*I'm just dreaming, so let me dream*
*I have a dream that the Bush will push the button*
*And it would backfire*
*And make his property tax higher*
*And put himself in financial limbo*
*Where he can't afford the gas to heat his pad*
*Fuel his jet, or his limo*
*And he'd have to roller skate to Kuwait, or Iraq, or Baghdad*
*Where ever the troops be at*
*And apologize for the lost lives*
*The suffering families, the pain and the hurt*
*And plant the seeds of soldiers dreams*
*Back in American dirt*
*I have a dream that poverty*
*Will finally be*
*a blurry past vision*
*And we can take the Ethiopian children*
*Off television*
*Cuz don't nobody really believe*
*We can feed*
*An entire village for the price of a cup of coffee*
*When we're struggling to feed our kids from Aldi*
*You might not admit it*
*But who are we kiddin'*
*I have a dream*
*That we would stop being idiots and hypocrites*
*And admit*
*If we put prayer back in schools*
*We could take metal detectors out*
*And Monday through Saturday*
*We can actually live Sunday's sermons out*
*And we'd really know the God that we're singin' about*

*In my sleep I heard myself singin' out*
*I felt the tears from my eyes streamin' down*
*If the deceased man can dream...and get us this far*
*Where can we go, if the living would start...*
*Dreaming*

# IF I HAD TIME

*If I had time*
*I would sit and write rhymes*
*In the rhythm of my own heart's beat*
*I'd paint a portrait of myself…*
*And call it Poetri*
*If I had time, I'd actually do*
*All the things that I've dreamed about*
*I'd be sight for the blind*
*And be the poor's way out…*
*Of the ghetto*
*If I had time*
*I wouldn't be so concerned*
*About money*
*Somebody told me, that time is money*
*And I don't have enough of either one…*
*If I had time, I'd have more fun*
*I'd make every night Sunday night*
*And every Monday morning, Saturday evening*
*Waiting for Sunday night one more time*
*If I had time…*
*I'd find my mind*
*Cuz' sometimes, it seems*
*I've lost it, or misplaced it*
*If I had time*
*I'd go to fear's door*
*Knock twice, and face it*
*If I had time…*
*I'd remind ya'll*
*That Jesus is soon to return*
*But no man knows the hour*
*Or is capable of comprehending*
*The fullness of His power*
*With His will, and His word…*
*We must fall in line*
*For as much as we think…*
*We have not enough time*

# I WRITE

*I don't have a voice without my pen*
*The poetry that I write and recite is the outlet*
*To unleash what's trapped within*
*I write to relay messages from God to men*
*Think it not strange*
*I'd rather be silent if what I say brings no change*
*So I write*
*I write for me and for you*
*I write for all we've seen*
*And all we go through*
*I write for single parents and families that ain't got enough food*
*I write for those who can't correctly express*
*The stress, that they face daily*
*I write for the little girl who don't know tell her mamma*
*She's havin' a baby*
*Especially since her baby daddy*
*Is her mamma's baby daddy…go figure*
*I write for the young boys who's pants sag as they brag on all the girls*
*They get*
*And the weed they smoke*
*As they choke*
*No one knows*
*About the tears they cry*
*They're afraid of not knowing how to be men…*
*So they have sex and get high*
*Instead of listening and hugging*
*We're eye-rolling and judging*
*We all realize change needs to take place*
*But let's face it*
*We're two faced if*
*We never take a step to make it*
*Change, that is*
*My soul is cryin'*
*Instead of sayin' one man can't change the world*
*Just change the world one man at a time*

*Try it…*
*If you can't say it…write it*
*Somebody told me that I can't write for nobody else*
*But my pen scribbles poetry from God's own breath*
*So I write*
*I write what everybody needs to hear but nobody wants to say*
*I write about ugly evils that won't go away*
*Until somebody's bold enough to stand up and say…*
*Get behind me satan.*
*I write things that I didn't even know I knew*
*As God speaks He tells me…*
*This isn't coming from you*
*Be not afraid, it's alright*
*Just write*
*Just jot down, then I'll blot out*
*All the transgressions of women and men*
*It's doesn't matter the sin…*
*It's all the same in My eyes*
*Tell every ear that hears*
*It was for them that I died*
*Then rose…*
*It was them that I chose…*
*That they might know*
*Me*
*No journey is too far, I'll come where ever they are*
*See,*
*I don't have a voice without my pen*
*The poetry that I write and recite is the outlet*
*To unleash what's trapped within*
*I write to relay messages from God to men*
*Think it not strange*
*I'd rather be silent if what I say brings no change*
*So I write*

## BLACK PEARL

*If you could be anything besides my mother*
*A black pearl is what you'd be*
*For a black pearl is priceless & rare*
*That's how you are to me*
*You possess the grace, beauty, & elegance of a dove*
*Because of you my life is filled with love*
*I credit you for making me who I am today*
*As for my appreciation…*
*There are no actions fit to show*
*No words great enough to say*
*The advice you give to me…*
*Makes the world's problems*
*As simple as the mind of a child*
*I find all the peace and tranquility I'll ever need*
*Each time I see you smile*

*I love you Ma…I truly thank you for everything*

# TRIBUTE

*Years ago God blessed the earth…*
*When He sent here your dear soul*
*I wish for all the joy and peace your tender heart can hold*
*May the stars hang a little lower tonight*
*So that every one is within your grasp*
*Take your time wishing upon each one*
*For anything you want…you can have*
*May love and wisdom guide your way*
*Lighting your path all the while*
*May your every day be as sweet, and beautiful*
*And as precious as your smile*
*In the Lord's garden you are a delicate flower*
*Fearfully, and wonderfully made indeed*
*For in your heart He's placed the things*
*That this world so desperately needs*
*Within you there is patience, understanding*
*Gentleness, & care*
*I've searched far & wide for the answers to life*
*In your eyes, I've found them there*
*Your presence brings with it calming whispers*
*Your touch never ceases to soothe*
*God has blessed the earth richly*
*By gracing it with you*

## TOMORROW

*Tomorrow I'll dream a dream of wonder*
*Just wait 'til tomorrow*
*Tomorrow I'll find a lover of lovers*
*Just wait 'til tomorrow*
*Tomorrow I'll dance in joy, & celebrate life*
*Just wait 'til tomorrow*
*Today I wait and peer through the window*
*For soon will come tomorrow*
*Tomorrow I will smile and jump and play and sing*
*Just wait 'til tomorrow*
*Tomorrow I will give freely and expect nothing in return*
*Just wait 'til tomorrow*
*Tomorrow I shall wish a stranger peace*
*Just wait 'til tomorrow*
*Today I think of yesterday*
*Realizing today…is already tomorrow*

# HEAVEN'S GATE

*When words escape my spirit*
*And silence settles in*
*When tears fall like rain*
*I hear your voice in the wind*
*Telling me as you always did…*
*That every thing's o.k.*
*As my memory rewinds*
*I do my best to try…*
*To remember all you had to say*
*Like the waters of the rivers*
*The wisdom of you words*
*Consistently flow*
*Reviving the rough dry places*
*Through prayers, and tears…*
*You nurtured me and watched me grow*
*Yet I can't find words beautiful enough to express exactly what you mean*
*The simplest way is just to say…*
*Thank you for everything*
*My heart misses you so…*
*To see you once more - I can't hardly wait*
*One day we'll be together forever more…*
*Just beyond Heaven's gate*

## SUPER WOMAN

*Bravery shines from your eyes*
*Strength illuminates from your soul*
*Beauty radiates from the essence of who you are*
*A woman with a heart of gold*
*Diamonds glitter in your smile*
*A graceful dance is your step*
*Precious and wonderful is your life*
*A gift from God is your breath*
*Surviving is not something you do*
*It's the characteristic of who you are*
*Your life is filled with purpose*
*And has been from the very start*
*Hope, & love, & joy, & peace*
*Are like the petals of roses*
*At your feet*
*Watching you live…*
*Enriches my life*
*As you conquer this battle*
*You've taught me to fight*
*As you stand strong against the blowing winds*
*I hold my head so high*
*For now I know that I too can win…*
*If at first I try*

# HUSTLE BY ANY MEANS

*We got poetry frames, special made cakes & CD's*
*We got socks, scented oils, & we do weaves*
*We got movies on boot leg…before they hit the theaters!*
*We got to move around to avoid all the haters*
*We got 24 hour day cares…& we baby-sit on the side*
*We quicker than cabs…call us for a ride*
*We do pedicures, arch eyebrows, & we do nails*
*We hustle by any means, but we do not sell tail!*
*We sell nachos out the kitchen, & rib dinners out the trunk*
*We sell the flyest authentic knock-offs…don't even front*
*Need an accountant, a counselor, a secretary, a maid?*
*We're women, we do this anyway…might as well get paid*
*We do washin' & ironin', so much we can handle*
*We sell make-up, real estate, & hand made candles*
*We got goals, hopes, & ambitions…*
*Daily we make life changing decisions*
*We got kids & bills, you know the deal*
*We know how to stretch a dollar, time, & a meal*
*We raise our children, we please our men, & we pursue our dreams*
*To all women…*
*African, Asian, Hispanic, Caucasian…*
*Hustle by any means*
*Need a house painted, a light fixed…*
*How about a massage…*
*We rotatin' tires, & changin' oil in the garage*
*What is it that you need…*
*We can do anything*
*We specialize in creative cash flow…*
*We hustle by any means!*

# AMAZING GRACE

*Amazing grace*
*The sound so sweet*
*The nation cheers and stands to it's feet*
*It's been a long time coming, but we've banished defeat*
*Finally manifested is Doctor King's speech*
*No longer a dream*
*It's the reality that breathes*
*Change has come for all who believe*
*Lifeless bodies limply hung from trees*
*We spent a lifetime of struggle planting seeds*
*That we may raise a nation like mighty oaks*
*Instill within them mighty hopes*
*Broken are the shackles, loosed are the ropes and*
*The window of opportunity is now wide open*
*For we've taken back our hopes and dreams*
*The last of the slaves, has finally been freed*
*No longer bound is our mentality*
*The truth that remains is the fact that we…*
*Are more than conquerors.*
*If nothing has yet…then nothing will ever conquer us*
*Equality for all men is now truth indeed*
*The soul of a man has no color or creed*
*Ours is the pursuit of happiness, life & liberty*
*Every man's right given liberally*
*Tears stream our faces as we face this*
*New day*
*The feeling is indescribable at the brink of change*
*Abolished is the falsehood of inferiority*
*Throughout the earth victory reigns*
*To God be the glory!*
*One nation under Him only, with liberty and justice*
*No way to apologize for such an injustice*
*All we ask now is that you simply respect us*
*The same measure you'd give yourself…*
*Give unto your fellow man*
*"I Have A Dream" is the vision*
*The promise is, "Yes We Can"*

# CHEERS

*Here's to a year of endless possibility, and opportunity that I will take advantage of*
*Here's to peace, joy, and real love*
*Here's to realizing my limits lie...within my own boundaries*
*My success is up to me, here's to me...giving myself to whomever is in need*
*The greatest among us served...and now it's my turn*
*Here's to last years tests, and trials, and hard lessons learned*
*Here's to more laughs, here's to life's forecast*
*Everyday might not be sunny, but everyday, it won't rain*
*Countless tears will fall...some from joy, some from pain*
*Here's to givin' it my best shot, givin' it all I got*
*Givin' it all to God*
*His faithfulness is great*
*Here's to Now...Life is too short to wait*
*The sky is the limit, is what they say*
*But I'm goin' far beyond*
*I can't stop at the stars, I'm reaching' for the Son*
*Not the solar system, but the only system for our entire existence*
*Here's to persistence...here's to faith that's gravity defying*
*If you tried and failed...just keep tryin'...keep cryin'*
*Those same tears will water your soul*
*What hurts you the most will help you to grow*
*Here's to growth and development...excuses are irrelevant*
*We must move forward...Here's to the birth of a dream conceived in a vision*
*Here's to starting a business*
*Here's to family...Here's to my sons, who are my soldiers*
*And my precious baby girl*
*Here's to realizing our children are next to run the world*
*Here's to Drae, Juan Jr., Des, and Vicki*
*Thankful, that they're still here with me*
*Here's to my husband who escaped a head on collision*
*Could have been a deadly car crash...*
*The air bags didn't inflate...*

*And he ain't got one scratch*
*Here's to God hearing the hearts of praying wives*
*I'm thankful for seat belts…*
*But Jesus saves lives*
*Here's to an Almighty God, for whom nothing is too hard*
*And here's to you…may you prosper in every area, may peace be yours forever, may*
*all your dreams come true…Here's to new beginnings*
*Let's pray and make change…if we do something different…*
*Our results won't be the same*
*Here's to us for w'ere destined to be great…*
*Here's to standing on the brink of a brand new day…*
*Seize the moment…*
*Here's to realizing time waits for no man*
*May you prosper beyond all you've done before*
*May the cup containing the sweetest nectar be yours*
*Here's to you…*
*Cheers-*

# SONGBIRD

*Songbirds with clipped wings*
*Don't sing…songs*
*They cry poems*
*Without the complication of a melody*
*Marching to a different drummer's beat is perfectly acceptable*
*I was never expected to*
*Take flight*
*I was raped by life and stripped of all my rights*
*So I don't write songs, I write wrongs, and call them poems*
*I got a voice, but it ain't pretty*
*I have no fancy colored feathers…my beauty is buried*
*Beneath the surface, beneath the hurts this world has dressed me in*
*You gotta look past my skin to see*
*Which means*
*Most of the people I meet will never notice me*
*I flutter through thick shadows…*
*I don't flourish in the light*
*Within my soul, I got rhythms and notes in every pitch and key*
*I'm still a songbird…I just got clipped wings*
*Too much pain, been hurt to too deep*
*I don't sing songs…*
*I cry poetry–*

## Soldier's Song

*Nobody can sing a soldier's song*
*Nobody else knows the words*
*No one can hum the melody to a song they've never heard*
*A soldier's song is written in trenches*
*On nights so dark and dreary*
*A soldier sings this song so proud*
*Through eyes so tired and teary*
*You see, a soldier's song is not mere words*
*Not simple melodies*
*The lyrics are written on mental images of how life use to be*
*This song echoes*
*From the bravery of the soul*
*Not the sound of the soldier's voice*
*Only a soldier knows that serving one's country is a duty*
*Not a choice*
*Soldier when you sing your song*
*Hold your head high and proud*
*Only a soldier has the strength*
*To sing*
*This kind of song out loud*

# Black Butterfly

*Through luminous beams*
*That seem*
*Too surreal for light*
*On jewel encrusted wings*
*Black Butterfly takes flight*
*Exploring new heights*
*Before never discovered*
*She flutters past invisible nets*
*That have been strategically set*
*To devise her demise*
*She survives fates that would under normal circumstances*
*Decrease her chances of flight*
*Her plight is too distinct this time*
*She remembers, & mimics, & imitates*
*Past gates that she was granted access to*
*Higher than the skies, wider than the miles*
*As she drifted through the impossible*
*With diamond eyes she winked at me*
*As if to make me think that I too*
*Could do that which she had done*
*I marveled at her strength & determination*
*Black Butterfly was my revelation*
*The realization that my flight was based*
*Solely on my decision to fly, or not to…*
*To move, or to stand still*
*To transform "I can't", to "I will"*
*Black Butterfly, inspires me to try to*
*Not only accomplish…*
*But be the master of all that I have dreamed*
*The beauty of her mystery*
*Intellect, integrity*
*The possibility she brings*
*Fluttering by*
*Flying high*
*On jewel encrusted wings*

# Chapter 5:
# Love

*This is the fragrance of "Passionate Passages". It is meant to bless, enrich, enhance, and celebrate husbands and wives. Romance to marriage, is like a flame to a candle. May yours always be lit…*

*Husband, this is for you, God has used you to heal my heart. It doesn't matter how many poems I write, somehow I can never find the words to express exactly what it is that I feel. The first love poem that I ever wrote was about you. The last one that I will ever write, will be about you. You have always been, and will always be…my love.*

*The most honest and complete words that come to mind are simply, "thank you…"*

*Love is patient, love is kind. It does not envy, it does not boast, it is not proud. It does not dishonor others, it is not self-seeking, it is not easily angered, it keeps no record of wrongs. Love does not delight in evil but rejoices with the truth. It always protects, always trusts, always hopes, always perseveres. Love never fails. But where there are prophecies, they will cease; where there are tongues, they will be stilled; where there is knowledge, it will pass away. (1 Corinthians 13:4-8)*

## DELICIOUS

When I'm with you
I feel like sunshine
Gravity has become non-existent
As I float on your kisses
Every time you hold me
Rain falls within my spirit
My flesh feels just
Like the petals of satin roses
I suppose this is
Why
The moisture of your kisses
Fills me with wishes
That can only be granted by you
I'm enchanted by you…
Delighted even
You leave me believin'
In the reality of dreamin'
Last night you left me silent
Completely speechless
You savored my lips
As if they dripped with the nectar of golden peaches
You selfishly indulged in my sweetness…
I finally felt the freeness
Of
What love was created to be
I in you
And you in me
And we no longer us
But one
Like the blazing heat
Of the rising sun
Our passion burns hotter than fire
You lifted me higher than elevation
I'll give all that you ask
With no hesitation

*For my whole life I've been waitin'*
*To feel just like this*
*Nothin' else fits the description*
*You lovin' me is...*
*Is simply delicious*

## OVERWHELMING

*More than the summer morning's sunrise*
*I love your eyes*
*I am intoxicated by your kiss*
*Your touch is overwhelming*
*You're like a piece of heaven right here on earth*
*Nothing compares to your worth*
*The way that I love you is indescribable*
*For years I have been trying to*
*Find words or ways*
*To express all the difference you've made*
*Since the first time you stepped into my world*
*You've helped me embrace the woman in me*
*For you've filled every void I had as a girl*
*Like a rosebud in spring...*
*You're love has blossomed me*
*I no longer day dream of fairytales*
*I live them...*
*I love you more everyday*
*I'm still amazed*
*That it's me that you love*
*I'll forever cherish every kiss and hug*
*You are truly irreplaceable*
*And I am indebted to you forever*

# FAIRYTALES

*Fairytales are not just for little girls*
*I know this much is true*
*A damsel in distress I once was…*
*That is, until I met you*
*You mean more to me, than words could ever describe*
*I fall in love all over at the meeting of our eyes*
*How could I not, when you are my rock*
*My strength, my heart, and soul*
*Supportive, forgiving, compassionate beyond measure*
*God blessed me with your hand to hold*
*You've taught me more about myself*
*Than I ever would have known*
*There is no way I could ever thank you…*
*Grateful, for all the love you've shown*
*So many ways you helped me to see*
*Visions beyond my view*
*In a world of uncertainties, one thing I know…*
*The best part of me, is you*
*You are my knight in shining armor*
*You are the man of my dreams…*
*I want you to know, had it not been for you*
*I would never have known what love really means*
*Thank you for taking the rain in my life*
*And using it to make me grow*
*I appreciate all that you are, and all that you've done…*
*And I thought that you should know*
*No matter how deep the trenches get*
*Or how high the mountains to climb*
*I know I'll make it through every storm*
*For there's a hero by my side*

# NOTHING

*Nothing makes me*
*Laugh and cry at the same time*
*For a million different reasons*
*Nothing*
*Nothing at all*
*Makes me fall*
*In love daily*
*I feel most like a lady*
*When you hold me*
*In your arms*
*I'm unfolding*
*Revealing who I am*
*No longer hiding*
*No longer pretending*
*Never before have I been*
*Free to be myself*
*But you've seen me*
*Unclothed, disrobed, beyond nude*
*No covering*
*Yet in love with me*
*Without changing*
*Surpassing the greatest of lovers*
*Exceeding the best of friends*
*From the beginning of time*
*Until the very end*
*My love will never*
*Belong to another*
*For there is nothing*
*No thing…*
*Nobody, like you*
*Only you*
*Nothing moves a woman*
*Nothing soothes a woman*
*Like love does*
*Nothing but love can make a woman*

*Remember not the sting of pain*
*Nor the anguish of despair*
*Only love*
*Can put butterflies in my hair*
*And stars in my eyes*
*Only love can decorate my thighs*
*With sighs*
*Which escape from your lips*
*As your mouth tastes the curves of my hips*
*You are incredible to me*
*I can't even find words to describe the high I get*
*Every time I get...*
*To be with you*
*Me and you*
*There's nothing better*
*Than love*
*Nothing better than us*
*Never knew life could be*
*So good*
*So pure*
*So true*
*Never knew love...*
*'Til I knew you*

## CAN I BE YOURS

If I asked if I could be yours
What would you say
By yours I mean with bodies intertwined
You put me to sleep every night
And with gentle kisses you wake me everyday
I want my hands to be the ones you hold when you pray
I want my smile to be your source of illumination
Throughout the day
Long hours after the sun has faded into the evening sky
My palms will hold each tear you cry
And I'll lift them before God as I pray for you
I'll ask Him for words of comfort to say to you
I'll ask Him to reveal secret things so I'll know
Just how to please you
I'll do what it takes so that every single day
You'll know how much I need you
More than all the riches of Solomon
My adoration for you goes beyond measure
More precious than gems or jewels
Any eye has ever seen
To have you love me is my treasure
I've only been in love once in my whole life
If God is love, than love never ends
There is no completion
Who can tell where it begins
It just exists, it's in your eyes, your touch, your kiss
I love you, none but God is above you
In the most secret place in my heart
That's how it's always been
Casting my pearls before swine
I spent years trying
To teach men…how to love me, spiritually
The way you naturally do
And you wonder why…
I always feel like, I wanna do more for you

*You don't even know it but you are more proof*
*That God hears my prayers*
*As for each tear that I've ever cried*
*The Father cares*
*The Master Craftsman has given me the genuine artifact*
*Of every emotional replica I've had before*
*And I'm just wondering what you would say...*
*If ever I were brave enough to ask...*
*Can I be yours*

# GOOD THING

*He who finds a wife finds a good thing*
*And obtains favor from the Lord*
*Every day as sure as I live*
*I love you more & more*
*In the morning, at the day's dawning...*
*You are my good thing*
*At noon, with thoughts of you my mind is consumed*
*You are my good thing*
*Late at night, you lay by my side*
*And the world seems right*
*You are my good thing*
*Your name is the song that my heart sings*
*Your voice is my melody*
*Your gentleness is my strength when I am weak*
*You are my good thing*
*Your laughter is like rain falling*
*Fresh and new*
*Everything that I need is inside of you*
*You are my peace in the storm, my joy in sorrow, my comfort in pain*
*Who can compare to you...*
*There is none other*
*Not only my wife, my best friend, my lover...*
*You are truly...*
*My good thing*

# LOVE

*Prophesies may fail, tongues may cease*
*Knowledge may go away*
*But Love will always be*
*Love is long suffering, humble, & kind*
*Love doesn't behave rude, or seek to please it's own mind*
*Love is not provoked, it has no evil thought*
*Love is a priceless treasure, it could never be sold or bought*
*Love is given freely, & freely it's received*
*It bears, hopes, endures, and believes all things*
*Love doesn't rejoice in iniquity, but only in the truth*
*Love is God, Himself in spirit*
*Dwelling inside of you*
*Love is looking into beautiful eyes, & seeing the brilliance of sparkling stars*
*Love is listening to your melodious voice, & hearing the song in your heart*
*Love is brave, it leads the soul*
*Fearlessly follow it blind*
*Love can not be contained*
*It will forever remain*
*Throughout all space & time*
*The strength & depth, & power of Love*
*One could never understand*
*To provide, protect, & hold a woman's heart…*
*For her, God made a husband*
*To support, encourage, & improve man's life…*
*From the rib of his side, God created a wife*
*Love is the whisper of God in the form of a breeze*
*Looking at you…*
*LOVE*
*Is what I see*

## MORNING AFTER

Last night we made love
And I knew, that something spiritual had taken place
As if in your heart I took my rightful place
As you kissed me soulfully
And held my face
Just like you use to
Back when I was new to you
We held each other so tight
So tender, so passionate
To be close wasn't enough
We melted into each other
You ministered to me and I to you
Fresh rain is what I feel like
I feel the peace and security of a new wife
You told me that your arms will only hold me
And if not me…
Then you'd stand alone
And I promise to make our house a happy home
A sanctuary, and a place of rest for you
I'll be everything you need
I'll do it just for you
Last night while we loved each other
I wanted to cry
Cuz there was a rebirth where part of me had died
I put down my guard and let you take control
A complete gentleman you are
Careful with my heart
Passionate with my soul
You sung songs in the whispers of "I Love You"
And my heart did dance
Not by chance
Cuz I have been waiting to feel like this
I've been patiently waiting to feel your kiss
We enjoy each other's taste
Irresistibly delicious

*And I don't want this to end*
*Cuz it's sacred like secrets between best friends*
*Like crushes between school aged kids*
*Like the glow of fireflies that light*
*My thighs*
*Inviting you to lose yourself beyond the boundaries of my garden*
*Where seeds are planted and flowers blossom*
*For your pleasure alone*
*I'm quiet with the exception of soft moans*
*Which emerge from deep within*
*Allowing you to see the vulnerable side of me*
*Such things for your eyes only*
*You look at me with amazement like*
*You did the first time*
*Before you touched my body, you embraced my mind*
*You held me like it was your last chance to*
*As we fell asleep…*
*This time your breathing was the melody*
*That my subconscious danced to*
*If I was speechless before*
*It's because I knew not the words*
*To express how deeply I love you…*

## SHE LOVES HIM

*He's so fine...*
*As she loses herself in his eyes*
*She wants to pause time*
*And live in a moment called...*
*Forever*
*No words could ever explain*
*How his kiss brings the rain*
*That washes all her pain*
*He soothes her beyond her wildest dreams*
*All she knows is that she loves him*
*Like a summer night's breeze*
*She loves him*
*Like fresh rain and warm sunshine*
*To the petals of golden roses*
*She needs him*
*When words tend to cease*
*And there are no more tears of grief*
*The sound of pleasure emerges from someplace deep*
*In a world they're forced to share*
*They feel like it's theirs...*
*Alone*
*She lays close to him, and softly moans*
*In his arms...*
*She feels like silk and lace*
*She's safe*
*He's replaced every awkward trait*
*And somehow made*
*Her life beautiful*
*And no matter how many poems she writes*
*Or songs she sings, or prayers she prays*
*He'll never know, to her...*
*What he really means*
*All she can ever tell him...*
*Is that she loves him*
*She knows not how to explain*

How easily she accepted pain
Cuz that's all she was use to
She knows he loves her more than he use to
He's so familiar, yet so much about him has changed
She's more than comfortable
She's one with him
And it feels so strange
He is the melody to her every lyric
In the stillness of the night…
You can hear it
As their heartbeats are in sync
Their inner rhythms compliment each other
He's a for real friend to her
And her passionate lover
He makes love to her
And re-creates the sunrise
He passes her every outer boundary
And disappears within her thighs
He concentrates on her body
And locks her soul
With his eyes
With no words, he reminds her…
That he loves her

## TIMELESS

*I waited a thousand years to hold you forever*
*Now that the moment has manifested itself as my reality*
*I'm never letting go*
*For each second that my eyes behold you*
*My arms wrap around you*
*My lips touch you*
*Feels like it's own eternity*
*Loving you has proved itself to be...*
*Timeless*

## MY LOVE

*I'm not exactly sure where life is going to take me*
*But I'll go as long as you come with me*
*I don't know what demands will be placed on me*
*But I'll do more than what is expected*
*As long as you have faith in me*
*I'll face the world and every problem attached to it*
*As long as I know when the day is done*
*You'll be there to hold me*
*When life's pressures cause me to lose myself in confusion*
*And my soul is bothered*
*I smile because I know I can find peace at the meeting of our eyes*
*Those times that I lay still beside you*
*Just know that I am speaking to God*
*Thanking Him for you and praying that as each day goes by*
*He'll strengthen our love for each other*

# JAZZ, CHOCOLATE COVERED STRAWBERRIES, & WINE

*I cordially invite you to spend a little time*
*An evening filled with stolen moments*
*To sit back and unwind*
*No interruptions*
*Just you & me…*
*Some jazz, chocolate covered strawberries & wine*
*We won't talk about work or children…*
*Right now bills don't exist*
*We'll get lost in each other's eyes*
*And find ourselves in each other's kiss*
*Rush to do nothing…*
*It's a must you take your time*
*This evening is ours*
*Just you & me…*
*Some jazz, chocolate covered strawberries & wine*
*Dim the lights*
*And light the candles*
*Perfectly set the mood*
*A fragrant mist*
*Among the sweetest kiss*
*A bubble bath for two*
*Release the stress, relax the tension, completely ease your mind*
*This time is ours*
*Just you & me*
*Some jazz, chocolate covered strawberries & wine*

# KNOW WHAT LOVE IS

*Not even in my wildest dreams*
*Have I ever imagined having a man like you*
*Love me*
*It's unconditional, more than physical, it's spiritual*
*Our life has been scripted*
*A love letter written*
*By God*
*With His own kiss it was sealed*
*Scribbled in eternity*
*To be eternally revealed*
*I never thought that someone like you would hold my hand*
*Helping me understand*
*Everything that was unknown*
*You've shown me so much about myself*
*You not only complete me, but you free me, you keep me reaching*
*You hold me while I'm sleeping, so when I'm finished dreaming*
*I wake to a reality more beautiful than anything subconsciously existing*
*You are too good to be true...you're unbelievable*
*We share a world with billions of people*
*Yet I feel like it's just me and you*
*You move me beyond every limitation I've been faced with*
*Let's face it*
*God uses you daily to show me what love is*
*And I'm grateful...*
*I thank you for choosing me to be she who keeps your heart*
*Rest assured*
*My every intention is pure*
*Loving you has always been natural for me*
*I do it without thinking*
*You've resuscitated a heart that ceased beating*
*Not having you would be like not breathing*
*You hold me in your arms, and my spirit sighs*
*When you kiss me, my soul cries*
*Cuz finally I...*
*Know what love is*

# MY SONG

*You are my soul mate*
*No one on earth can make me feel*
*The wonderful way that you do*
*My spirit smiles*
*I'm over-joyed*
*Every time I think of you*
*You complete me, you free me*
*You make me whole*
*Your love is a spiritual symphony…*
*You are the song in my soul*
*And I sing you…*
*You are the melody to my every lyric*
*The very breath that you breathe*
*Keeps rhythm with my heart's own beat*
*You are music to me…*
*And I dance to you continuously*

# TO BE LOVED BY YOU

*No chocolate is sweeter than your kiss*
*No flower is more beautiful than your face*
*Nothing on earth has enough worth...*
*To ever take your place*
*You are my Valentine*
*My Fourth of July...*
*My Christmas Morning*
*You're New Year's kiss*
*At the strike of midnight*
*Not only are you my birthday...*
*You are the icing on the cake*
*You are my special occasion*
*And I celebrate you daily*
*Tell me what it is that I can do for you...*
*To make you feel the way that I do*
*I want you to think of my eyes*
*And smile*
*The way that I do, when I think about yours*
*I want you to experience a joy*
*That you've never felt before*
*I want you to lose track of time*
*The way that I do*
*I want you to know what it feels like...*
*To be loved by you*

# SO COLD

I want to write a poem so cold
It'll make the devil want to sell his soul
Back to Christ, twice
That's two times
I wanna find words that rhyme with your name
So I can say "Juan" at the end of each line
I want this poem to be so cold
It will freeze all of creation
And completely stop time
Nothing will move, but the spirit of God, me, and you
Let's see how it would be then
Maybe for us, He'd recreate the garden of Eden
Since we already know what was foretold to you and me
I'd never give you the fruit from the forbidden tree
Instead, I'd let you feast on me
We'd be the millennium version of Adam and Eve
Only this day…
We be known as Juan and Tee
I wanna write you a poem so cold
When spoken, heard, or read…
It would cause frost bite
I want it to feel like it has a wind-chill of a hundred below at midnight
And only two degrees warmer during daylight
I want this poem to be so cold
It replaces cubes of ice
You'll find yourself puttin' my poetry in your glass of sprite
Cuz' you want it just that cold
I want to write you a poem so cold
It'll make an igloo feel like a castle made of sand
Even though it's my love that warms you…
You'll get chills when you touch my hand
I want this poem to be so cold
No one can comprehend it but you and I
I mean, I want this poem to make it snow in July
I want this poem to freeze your tears

*Before they ever leave your eyes*
*If not for love, then I don't want you to cry*
*I want this poem to be the cause for hell freezin' over*
*I know it sounds insane…*
*But I want this poem to actually freeze flames*
*I wanna write you a poem so cold it will make every other poem ever*
*written*
*Non-existent*
*I want this poem to be so cold*
*The deaf will hear it*
*The blind will read it in Braille and receive sight*
*I want this poem to give you braggin' rights*
*You can tell every other brother that my love poems to them*
*Were really like poems*
*They got all the left overs, and you get all the right poems*
*Looking at you makes me wanna write poems*
*You're one of God's greatest works of art…*
*You're just that fine*
*Since I'm Poetri…*
*And I'm yours*
*I want you to take my hand and declare…*
*This poem is mine*
*For you, I'd be the coldest poem ever*
*I'm determined to write this poem and I won't drop this pen*
*'til I'm thru…*
*My goal is to somehow write a poem*
*That's as cold…*
*As you*

## TO BE WITH YOU

*More beautiful than any lyric ever sang*
*More breath taking than any note ever played*
*Is simply the way...*
*You look at me*
*Not even the first breeze of spring*
*Compares to your stare*
*I'm captivated and amazed*
*Caught in your gaze*
*There's something about the way...*
*You look at me*
*Your eyes look past mine*
*As you stare at a soul*
*Once paralyzed*
*Since the day you came*
*Into my life*
*I've*
*Been able to focus*
*Clear is my view*
*Life is so much more beautiful*
*Standing next to you*
*God heard the secret prayers that I prayed*
*Like flowers, He collected my desires*
*And for me, He made...*
*You*
*Nothing more could I ever ask*
*Than to be with you*
*For only you could complete me*
*Only you could make me whole*
*Today we are no more two...*
*But one*
*In body, mind and soul*
*One of the greatest joys I've ever known*
*Is the pleasure of being with you...*

# *Alabaster Box*

*Tisha Leija was born as Nartisha Maineke Jemison on November 12th 1976. She was born and raised in Milwaukee Wisconsin. She discovered her love for poetry in the second grade. Leija recalls checking out Shel Silverstein's "A Light In the Attic", a book of children's poetry from her elementary school library each week. As a child Leija found great joy in writing short stories. She was invited several times the Young Author's Conventions. Before middle school was already a published author. She has always been able to clearly express her ideas in writing. Like most little girls, she wrote daily entries in her journal. Out of "concern" her mother read her journal. That is when Leija began to write in what she deemed to be "code", but actually it was the birth of a poet. "I just wanted to write so that even if she did read it, she wouldn't understand what I was saying. What I found was greater than that. The more I wrote, the better I understood myself."*

*Writing became an outlet for her, no matter what the situation…with a pen, some paper, and a moment of solitude she was able to sort out whatever situation she encountered.*

*Tisha Leija graduated from Homestead High School in 1995. In her teen years, her friends would read what she wrote and ask her to write letters of love on their behalf. Her school mates would tell her how they felt about someone special and Leija would compose beautiful poetry as if it had been written directly from the heart of the person giving the poem. As an adult she created a business doing this exact same thing. She opened a specialty*

139

*store in downtown Milwaukee called Lyrics by Leija. Her customers would express their feelings and Leija was able to capture not only what they said, but what they couldn't find the words to say. She created keepsake gifts by artistically framing her work. She has written for every stage of life, for many different people. For a time, she was a weekly feature on a popular Milwaukee radio station. Leija remembers, "A man came into my shop very arrogantly announcing that he too was a writer. He looked around my boutique, then down at me and told me that it's impossible to write for anyone else. I laughed and thought to myself..."I guess I've been doing the impossible for years."*

*In her early twenties she found great pleasure in going to open mic nights. Each week she would have a chance to recite her work in a room full of people who shared the same love for poetry as she did. At that time no one knew who she was by name. She was simply introduced as "Poetri".*

*Leija says that she knows that her gift of writing is special and that it's from God. "It's something that I can just do. It's already there...I just have to let it flow. The Lord speaks to my heart, all I do is write what I hear. I take no credit for what I write. I give all glory to God. As Awesome as He is, he takes time to talk to me...*

*My heart is overflowing with a good theme;*
*I recite my composition concerning the King;*
*My tongue is the pen of a ready writer.*
*(Psalm 45:1)*